Internal Drive Theory®:
Motivate Your Child to WANT to Study

Internal Drive Theory®:
Motivate Your Child to WANT to Study

Dr Petunia Lee

To the father of Little Boy and The Daughter

Contents

1 | The First Chapter

This chapter aims to convince you that internal drive for school work can be developed. It is not an inborn trait. We can cultivate it in our children. We just need to know how. This book is written from both my experience as a mother, and as a consultant-researcher in the field of employee motivation. As I researched into employee motivation, I worked with organisations to analyse motivational issues in their teams. I also worked with managers to help them improve their motivational strategies. Very naturally, I also applied the same motivational principles to my own children, with excellent results.

In 2012, I started to run One-to-Pair Motivation Therapy™ sessions for parent-child pairs. I had not planned to do these sessions. It was simply that so many parents with un-motivated kids had emailed me for advice. I started off by spending hours explaining the strategies to parents on the phone. Invariably, they would nod their heads and claim that they had understood. However, when we crossed paths again sometime later, they would explain to me that there was something wrong with the child, and the strategies had not worked. I scratched my head. Was there really something wrong with their child (or the strategies)? The strategies were developed from decades of documented research done by eminent psychologists in both labs and organisations. They worked with my kids. I was curious as to why they had not worked for other people's kids. It was hard for me to believe that that my children were somehow born superior to other people's children. I also wondered about the effectiveness of the strategies.

To investigate, I invited each parent-child pair to my home, and then I personally used the same strategies on other people's children. In every case, the child responded to me positively. One child's Father assured me that his son would never be able to focus if I insisted on getting the Primary 4 boy to memorise Chinese compositions of

Secondary 3 level. The Father said, "There is something wrong with my son. I am bringing him to a cognitive psychologist for testing." After about 1.5 hours of working with me, the little one had already completed almost half of the Secondary 3 composition. Then, I turned and gloated at the Father.

On another occasion, a Mother came to me for help to motivate her daughter in the face of challenge. The Mother said "My daughter runs away from challenge. Given a choice, she will always choose the more easy work to do. Prior to the One-to-Pair Motivation Therapy™ session, the Mother sounded sceptical on the phone. She gently explained to me that her daughter would probably respond better to me because I was a stranger. Hence, it may have nothing at all to do with effective motivation strategies. The Mother explained, "You're not her Mother so she won't dare to refuse to do your challenging work." Halfway through the session, the Mother's jaw dropped when her Primary 4 daughter insisted on completing a Primary 5 problem sum even after I had said, "I know this is difficult. Would you like to go back to easier work?" This was more than just mere obedience to a stranger. This was a stubborn desire to face challenge without giving up, even when given a choice to give up. Again, I had the chance to gloat at the Mother and I did that with some understandable gusto.

I am not writing these words to show off. I am writing them in an attempt to convince parents that the strategies in this book can work on children who didn't inherit genes from my husband and myself. The more One-to-Pair Motivation Therapy™ sessions I run, the more I am convinced that if the child is un-motivated, it is not because there is something wrong with the child. Instead, there is something wrong with the adult who has care of the child.

I say the above hesitantly. I may one day meet a child that is genetically programmed to be un-motivated, and thus none of the motivation strategies I normally use would work on that child. It can happen. I can't say for sure it won't. I can only say with certainty that after running so many One-to-Pair Motivation Therapy™ sessions, I have yet to meet this child. However, I have met many parents who don't know how to motivate.

MY KIDS WEREN'T BORN WITH HIGH INTERNAL DRIVE
My friends tell me I have weird children. My son went visiting with homework in hand, found a quiet corner and

finished his homework whilst everyone else was yelling circles around him. Everybody thought I had made him do that, but I hadn't. In fact, I had actually objected to him packing his homework for the visit. My teenage daughter and I used to get into huge fights because she studied too hard. Some days, I wanted to keep her home because she looked too ill to go to school, but she sulked and insisted to get up at 5.30 am, bleary-eyed and snotty-nosed in order to attend school.

People tend to believe that such children are born that way. I can assure you that mine were not. In Primary 1, The Daughter scored in the bottom 25% of her year. In Primary 2, 3 and 4, she was very inconsistent. She would score averagely well at those Continual Assessments when I sat with her to study. However, no matter how much effort I put in, she never scored brilliantly.

Does that sound familiar to you?

It came to a point where my husband and I shook our heads and told ourselves that we had a daughter with limited IQ. We told ourselves to accept that fact graciously whilst focusing on cultivating her other qualities. Then, I began serious research into the science of human motivation as part of my doctoral studies. Naturally, I experimented on my child with the following results.

The Daughter made it to an excellent all girls' school. In Secondary 3, she was one of the 25 students in her year picked to form a class created to develop talent in the specific niche area of her strengths. She was a student leader, and a prize-winning competitive sports girl. In Secondary 1 and Secondary 2, she did not rank below 3rd position in her class. The Husband and I now know that her poor academic results in primary school were due to a lack of internal drive, not a lack of intelligence.

Once we had successfully ignited her internal drive, she simply powered herself forwards and reached destinations that we had never envisaged for her. We did not even know that her secondary school had special classes for developing talent in niche areas. Thus, we could not help her aim for them. She herself decided what she wanted to do, and she worked hard to get into that class.

I started researching into the science of human motivation as part of my own development in Human Resource Management consulting. I began by reading the research done mainly in industrial and organisational psychology, and then I crossed over to read educational psychology, and even some health psychology. Then, I conducted my own research. Through my children's growing years, I applied my learning to managing their academic journey through Singapore schools.

This is the story of my children's journey from "being forced to study" to "wanting to study", and what I did to get them from one point to the other. I hope that this book will bless children more than parents because much is expected of Singaporean children, and if the parent can better motivate towards success, the child will have a less painful childhood.

I write this book because too many Singaporean children are hurting.

2

About Internal Drive Theory®

Inspired by the work of Professor Edward L. Deci and Professor Richard M. Ryan.

The set of motivational strategies I will be describing in this book are grouped under an internationally trademarked term, registered under the Madrid System for the International Registration of Trademarks – "Internal Drive Theory®". From the perspective of Internal Drive Theory®, motivation is defined as "how much internal drive an individual has to do something".

- Do you study because you are forced to?
- Or do you study because you think it is important?
- Or do you study because you love it?

In the first case, you have very low internal drive. You are externally pushed/forced/coerced by someone or something to study. In the second case, you have a moderate level of drive. In the last case, you have very high levels of internal drive. These three levels are illustrated in Figure 2.1.

I study because…

My mother wants me to.	I feel it is important.	I enjoy it.

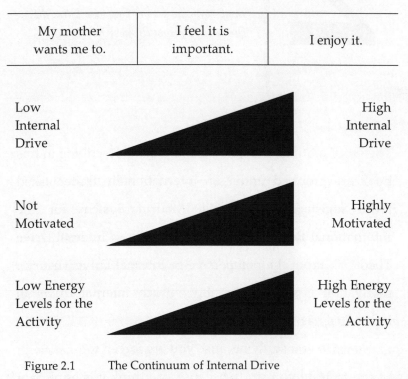

Low Internal Drive	High Internal Drive
Not Motivated	Highly Motivated
Low Energy Levels for the Activity	High Energy Levels for the Activity

Figure 2.1   The Continuum of Internal Drive

Let us now try to understand each of the three levels of drive depicted in Figure 2.1 above. They are

　　Level 1: I study because my mother wants me to.

♀   Level 2: I study because I feel it is important.
♀   Level 3: I study because I enjoy it.

LEVEL 1: I STUDY BECAUSE MY MOTHER WANTS ME TO

A child who studies only when he is made to, doesn't really want to study. If the parent does not push, the child does not study. One practically needs to be monitoring the child at all hours, or get others to do so. This is exhausting for parents. If your child is at this level of drive, he is un-motivated.

LEVEL 2: I STUDY BECAUSE I FEEL IT IS IMPORTANT

A second reason why we may do things is that we feel they are important. Parents take leave to study with their children because they feel it's important to be there. This depth of feeling comes from the deep love many parents feel for their offspring. I save money in the bank for my retirement because I feel it's important to be financially secure in my old age. This depth of feeling comes from a childhood experience wherein my family's fortunes went through lean times. I grew up somewhat insecure about money, and as a result, I deeply feel the importance of saving.

Do note that I have used the word "feel" not "think". For those of us who pride ourselves in being rational, let's face it. Motivation is not about the logical mind. It is about the willingness of the heart. It is about feeling like you really, really want to get something done. It is feelings, not logic, that provide internal drive. Many people think that saving money is important, but unless you grew up in circumstances where your family had no money to buy you new clothes, you might not deeply feel the importance of saving money.

If logic did motivate, then Singaporean food courts would not be full of people stuffing their faces with lard laden foods such as *char kway teow* and *chye tow kueh* (two sinful Singaporean culinary delights). These people know that lard will clog up their arteries but it feels so good to indulge! Not until some of these people are felled by a heart attack do they begin to feel the importance of avoiding lard. This is why you can reason all you want with your child about the importance of a good education, about not growing up into the garbage collection profession, about avoiding the fate of the road sweeper... it won't motivate the child because reason appeals to logic. The child understands but does not feel the deep

conviction that you feel. If, however, the child deeply feels
the importance of studying, then the child's internal drive
for studying would be moderately high. In this book, I will
share strategies on how to help a child to feel the
importance of a good education.

LEVEL 3: I STUDY BECAUSE I ENJOY IT

There are some things in life that we do because we enjoy
them. I experience a lot of drive for gardening simply
because I enjoy gardening. I feel quite energetic when I
wake up before the sun has come up, and think to myself
"Ah! I can spend the whole morning weeding and pruning
in my garden." Other people I know will walk for 4 hours
in the blistering hot sun with a heavy bag full of golf clubs,
hitting a little white ball from one hole to another. They too,
wake up before dawn and say "Hooray! I can spend my
whole morning hitting a little white ball in the hot sun."
Restaurants are filled with people who feel internally
driven to pay through the nose, in order to put stuff into
their mouths. If it is something we enjoy, we have a lot of
drive. In some parts of this book, I will also show you how
you can get a child to enjoy something he/she didn't at first
enjoy.

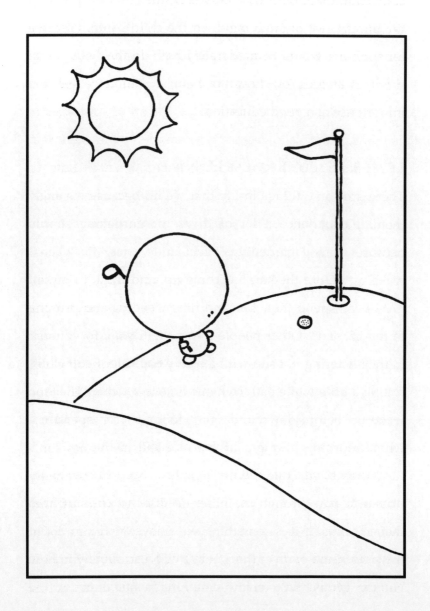

CAN INTERNAL DRIVE BE DEVELOPED?

We all can feel internal drive, or the lack thereof. Yet, we cannot see it. Since we cannot see it, it is difficult to imagine that we can actually control and enhance its development. Past generations, before us, attributed rain to supernatural causes. However, nowadays, we know how to make it rain (by cloud seeding), and people like me, know how to develop internal drive. Yes... it is possible to bring a child from being forced to study, to enjoying their studies. I call this process "Internal Drive Ignition™".

Many children have their drive ignited by a random set of circumstances. Perhaps their parents have done something right, but they don't know what they've done right. Perhaps the child has come into contact with a very special teacher, or tutor. The randomness of Internal Drive Ignition™ is such that people can't explain why and how it happens, and so they say "The child is born that way."

I only have two children. Knowing what I know about human motivation, I was not about to leave their Internal Drive Ignition™ to random chance. I have tried and tested the strategies I learnt in the course of obtaining my PhD in Human Motivation, on my children. In fact, some of the strategies that I will be sharing as part of Internal Drive

Theory®, have been used in

- healthcare, where Professor G.C. Williams and his colleagues helped doctors, nurses and therapists to enhance obese people's internal drive for losing weight[3].

- schools, Professors W.S. Grolnick and R.M. Ryan examined how parents played a part in increasing the internal drive of their children for schoolwork[4].

- organisations, where Professors K.M Sheldon and A.J. Elliiot examined how employees' internal drive for work can be enhanced[5].

So you see, I'm not writing about strategies that I made up. My contribution with this book is how I have pulled strategies from different streams of motivation research and used them to help children. Since the entire basket of strategies is meant to enhance internal drive, I have brought them all together under the umbrella term of Internal Drive Theory®.

THE IMPORTANCE OF INTERNAL DRIVE IGNITION™

This book isn't about how to teach children Math, English, Chinese or Science. There are many courses and books already designed for that purpose. There are many tuition centres offering programmes on how to teach Creative Writing or Math Heuristics. This book aims to address the more intangible issue of Internal Drive Ignition™.

One very important reason for igniting their drive in primary school is that when children reach secondary school they become harder to push. As children move into secondary school with their internal drive still left un-ignited, it soon becomes impossible for parents to push them in any way. This is the age of rebellion, remember? In primary school, most children are still relatively docile. After the PSLE (Primary School Leaving Examinations - Singapore's nationwide examinations for 12-year-olds), it gets harder to make them do what you think they should do. If parents have pushed their children hard (and incorrectly) since Primary 1, some children come already to the end of their tether in Primary 5 or 6. They will rebel. If your child digs in his heels and ignores your attempts to help him do well in the PSLE, he will jeopardise his own chances at the PSLE. In other families, parents manage to stave off the age of rebellion till secondary school. Their children make it through to good secondary schools on the strength of tutor and parental drive. In secondary school,

17

these same children strive for independence. They will do the opposite of what they know is important to you, simply because they feel the natural psychological urge to differentiate themselves from their parents. They want to grow into their own persons, and not remain extensions of their parents. If their success at the PSLE has been largely due to parental drive, such children will rebound and go in the other direction. They will fight their parents' every effort to help them score good grades. Once they reject your attempts to help them, their grades will dip. One parent shared on the kiasuparents forum (www.kiasuparents.com) that her child told her point blank that Math and Chinese are useless and that he was not interested in going to Secondary 2 at all[*].

Children who succeed because of parental drive in primary school, postpone the day when they must learn to power their way forwards by themselves. Children who are used to relying on the engines of parents in primary school can lose steam in secondary school when faced with all the other challenges of adolescent emotional upheaval. Trying to find success in a time of adolescent upheaval is a

---

[*] www.kiasuparents.com/kiasu/forum/viewtopic.php?f=23&t=27910

challenge we can help our children overcome, if we make sure we ignite their internal drive for school early, by the end of Primary 4.

The second reason why it makes sense to ignite internal drive, is that performance is very much enhanced. In a way, it is like pushing a car. A very strong man, like a very domineering parent, can push a Ferrari around. However, no matter how strong the man, or how domineering the parent, unless the Ferrari itself provides an internal drive, it can never go from zero to 100km/h in 7.2 seconds flat. Imagine that your child has the potential of an academic Ferrari. Wouldn't it be a pity to have to keep pushing him to study? No matter how hard driving you may be, your beloved little Ferrari of schoolwork would drive himself or herself far harder than you ever could. Even if your child does not have the potential of a Ferrari, but has instead, the sensible potential of a Toyota Vios, he would still move faster if the drive came from within him, than from you.

OUR BIKE TURNED OUT TO BE A FERRARI
After Internal Drive Ignition™, The Daughter not only met but also repeatedly surpassed our

expectations of her. We simply wanted her to do well enough to get into a good secondary school. She did that, and then went on to win academic prizes every year. In addition, she competed and won for her school in sports. Later, she was selected into an academic program for niche talent development. Eventually, she graduated with 8 distinctions at the 'A' levels.

The two people who are most surprised are her father and I. I remember feeling so depressed at her report card in Primary 1. It was so much effort to have to sit by her after I came home from work every night. Every night, my blood pressure went up whilst she sat there miserable and crying in front of me.

There came a point when we seriously thought that she only had the potential of a bicycle. The Husband and I comforted ourselves and hoped that she would marry well. Instead, she turned out to be something of a Ferrari herself, pushing her limits where I do not myself dare to push her.

3 | Structured Choices

Inspired by the work of Professor Edward L. Deci and Professor Richard M. Ryan.

WHAT ARE STRUCTURED CHOICES?

I use the term "structured choices" to refer to a selection of choices that are acceptable to you, as the parent. For example, I didn't allow Little Boy to choose whether or not to do his homework. Instead, he was allowed to choose between completing his homework before, or after, his bath. Or, he could choose which piece of homework to start on.

Kids at any age can be given choices. This is such a simple thing to do that us parents fail to appreciate its subtle effects on the child's psychology. Basically, humans are hardwired with a need to feel in control. Even little humans respond positively to being given a small degree of control over their lives. To protect them and guide them

21

however, we dare not give them broadly unstructured choices such as how to spend their days. We can, however, provide choices bounded by what is acceptable to us and not harmful to them. Here are some examples of the choices I gave Little Boy when he was in Primary 3:

1. How many problem sums from this assessment book do you think you can manage – three, four or five?

2. Here are six English exams from different schools. Would you like to choose one to do tomorrow morning when mommy is at work?

3. Here are three picture compositions. Which one would you like to do?

WHY GIVE STRUCTURED CHOICES?

The moment the child makes a work goal choice, he makes an unconscious commitment to focus on that work goal. This means that the child will be more likely (though it is no guarantee) to sit at the table and carefully complete the work goal he has chosen, even if you have left the house to go to a dinner party. Such goal focus and goal commitment has been shown in motivation research to enhance performance at work and at tasks[6]. Next, having freely

made his choice, the child's mind naturally rationalises the decision. Why did I choose to do this? There can only be two answers to that question. First, I chose to do it because it is important (Level 2 internal drive). Second, I chose to do it because I like it (Level 3 internal drive). This semi-conscious rationalisation of choices has the following effect. The child begins to believe that the work he has chosen to do is either important, or enjoyable.

How this strategy works can be understood from the perspective of psychological research in cognitive dissonance. Cognitive dissonance is the puzzled tension that comes after you choose to do something you know you would not normally do. Your mind naturally moves to get rid of cognitive dissonance by rationalising your action. In this way, children would convince themselves that they study because they like it (or think it important) simply because they need to rationalise why they chose to study. See the following Side Note Box for more explanation.

When you provide structured choices to your child, you actually get him to choose to do work. This is something that the child normally wouldn't choose. At the same time, a young child would not have experienced enough unpleasantness in education to violently reject

A Side Note: Cognitive Dissonance

In 1959, Professor Festinger set up a psychological experiment where he made subjects spend one hour turning wooden knobs[1]. It was the most boring activity Professor Festinger could devise. After one hour of this boring activity, subjects were asked if they would help to lie to the next participant (who was just an actor) about how interesting and enjoyable the activity was.

Imagine that you are the subject. You're in a scientific experiment and you're paid either $10 or $200 to take part. Since the researcher asked nicely, you agree to help tell the lie. The next participant (who is actually an actor) comes in and you say "It was a delightful experience. You will enjoy it." The actor responds "Really? My friend took part and he was bored to tears." You stop for a while and then you say "No... no... It really is quite interesting. Quite fun."

Now, if you were only paid $10 and you chose to help lie that the activity was interesting, you would feel a lot of cognitive dissonance because $10 is hardly enough justification to lie. Your puzzled psyche will try to find a reason for your choice. The only reason left for choosing to say it was interesting is that it really was interesting. So, you begin to believe that it really is interesting.

The results of the experiment showed that those paid the equivalent of $10 to say the activity was interesting rated it more interesting than those subjects paid $200. Why? Because those who were paid $200 had good reason to explain why they lied – money. Those paid almost nothing had no good reason to lie, and so they made themselves believe that it really was interesting.

doing work altogether. The child doesn't particularly want to work but neither does the child have strong objections to doing work. This relative neutrality towards work can be turned into internal drive for schoolwork, or if the parent is not careful, it can turn later to an intense dislike of schoolwork. How you provide the choices is as important as the choices you provide.

Put a Primary 1 child on your knee and ask nicely that he choose any one of three work options. If he refuses all of the three, then you offer others (perhaps other subjects, or other work tasks in the same subject). He only needs to make the first choice and that will allow you to suggest a reason for a choice that your child knows is against his natural instinct. You can suggest "I am so proud of you. You chose to do this piece of work. You must either be a boy who enjoys work or you're a very responsible boy who thinks work is important." Your young child's puzzled psyche will then consider these two reasons for having chosen what it would not normally choose.

As your child makes work choices daily, days will run into months. Months will run into years. Soon, he will change his attitude towards work. He will begin to believe that work is halfway fun, and he will begin to believe that it is important. However, this single strategy is not enough. Motivation is like water. To contain and harness water requires multiple structures. To contain and harness your child's motivational energy requires more than a single strategy. Read on to other chapters to get familiar with these other strategies.

THE CHALLENGES OF PROVIDING STRUCTURED CHOICES

Challenge 3.1: Forcing a Child to Do Something Is Easier

Adults hold absolute power over children. It is so easy to tell a small child what to do and then to have him do it. From the perspective of a child, the adult is a very large animal. An insistent full-grown adult can force a child to do anything. It is so easy to just MAKE your child do what you want. As a result, it takes a lot of parental self-control to structure choices for children. Yet, even little people respond well to being allowed to choose amongst a few options. Getting to choose from a selection of options also starts the child on the road towards developing good judgment for making wise choices later.

Challenge 3.2:   Being Sincere

Children are sensitive to parental pressure. If you are any

less than sincere, it will be coercion. For some children, a slight disapproving look is enough to achieve this coercive effect. Hence, unless you have thought through the various choices you are providing, and are truly comfortable with all the choices you are offering, unwitting coercion is a real danger. Let me illustrate the challenges of structuring choices for children with a family anecdote.

A Trip To The Library

The strange thing about our family is that my husband is more comfortable with Chinese than English, whilst I am more comfortable with English than Chinese. It sometimes almost feels like a cross-cultural marriage. As a result, The Husband was in charge of inculcating a love for Chinese literature in our children, and I had the charge of inculcating a love for English literature. Each of us aimed to instil an interest in reading the target language simply because everybody knows that to score well in languages at the PSLE, the child must read a lot.

Little Boy loved English and hated Chinese. The Husband was aware that structured choices

28

worked very well with his children. He had seen
me give them structured choices with good
results. The Husband himself tried to provide
structured choices too. However, he is an
impatient man.

He walked Little Boy very quickly over to
the library. He quickly pulled out Chinese
books that he thought suitable, and then he
spread them out on the floor in front of my
son, saying in a tight and urgent voice "Do you
like this one?" and "Do you like this one?"
Before Little Boy could answer, my husband
said "This is very good and interesting!", and
before my son could counter, my husband said
"How about this one?" And without pausing
much, my husband then said impatiently,
"Choose! Which book do you want!? Choose!"

Many children have an intuitive mastery of
body language and facial expression. Little Boy
could tell the father's barely concealed
impatience. It was almost as if my husband was
shouting into the Grand Canyon "You MUST
like Chinese" and the echoes of his father's

unspoken command reverberated unendingly around my son's head. The poor child didn't feel that he had a choice. He knows he MUST like Chinese books and the result was that he hated them.

Now, let me describe how I managed to get Little Boy addicted to English books. Up until Primary 2, my son didn't particularly enjoy reading. He read with some degree of competence, but he wouldn't pick up a book unless he was told to. When his first English exam came back, his teacher commented that it would help to read more. And so began the trips to the library. I let him browse for books that he liked. I too went around picking out books that I thought he might like. He came back with some choices that he thought were great because they were thin and full of pictures. I said, "No, no. Don't borrow baby books because you're not a baby anymore. You're a big boy." On my end, I sometimes went to him with choices that he thought were boring, "Mom, I don't like this. It's all about yucky fairies."

The aim, we both knew, was to agree on four books. Every time I found a suitable book, I would say, "Can you read a bit of this and let me know if you want to read the rest?" I provided him with a real choice, and if he said he didn't like the book, I didn't insist. Sometimes I felt like insisting but I controlled the urge to impose my will on him. After all, since I was already imposing my will insofar that I absolutely required him to read four books, I could very well accept that he choose the four books he wanted to read. It took us longer to choose books because we needed to discuss and negotiate. It took some self-control on my part but he went home feeling like a big boy because he had been trusted to choose his own books. And I was happy because I was comfortable with all his choices. Sometimes, he would realise that he actually didn't like a book we had borrowed and I respected his choice there too.

At first, he read the books he had chosen

because in choosing the books, he had already convinced himself that they were halfway fun. Then one random morning, just before the mid-year exams in Primary 2, he picked up a Secret Seven book without being told to, because he was bored and looking for some halfway fun. He was so captivated that he only answered me in monosyllables that whole morning.

Seeing his absorption in a book, I decided to strike whilst the iron was hot. I proposed then and there to bring him to the bookstore after lunch to buy the whole series of Secret Seven books. We came home with the entire series of The Spiderwick Chronicles, Secret Seven and Famous Five. Never had I bought him so many possessions at one go. Then, we went for a nice lunch and had a marvellous day walking down Orchard Road. The day stood out in Little Boy's memory as completely unforgettable and sweet.

Notice in this story that I first structured his choices.

Then I respected his choices. And when he finally freely made a choice that I completely approved of, I supported his choice in such a spectacular way that he felt pure exhilaration. On that fateful morning just before his Primary 2 mid-year exams, when he freely chose to read an English book for pleasure, I added to his pleasure and turned it into intense joy. This intense joy imprinted into his psyche, an association between pleasure and reading.

The library and the bookstore is a wonderful place to offer structured choices. There are just thousands of books to choose from.

Challenge 3.3: Offering Choices with Just the Right Degree of Freedom

Parents, by the time they become parents, have quite forgotten how to think like children. Every grown man has forgotten that every little boy believes that play gives infinitely more bang for the minute than work. Until you have gotten your child to believe that work is important and half way fun, you shouldn't be offering widely autonomous choices such as "Would you like to do any work today?" If your child chooses play over work in response to a question, it is not because there is something wrong with your child, it is because you have not succeeded in developing in your child a sufficient degree of internal drive such that he feels the importance of doing work and/or feels it is halfway fun. So, when can you risk giving your child widely autonomous choices? The following 2 anecdotes illustrate.

To Work or NOT to Work

At the end of his Primary 5 year, our family went for a holiday in Tasmania. Since Little Boy had worked hard the whole year, it really didn't matter to me if he didn't choose to study whilst we were in Tasmania. However, I decided to make the most out of even this occasion to build internal drive.

I contrived to ask him if he would like to bring his Primary 6 *ting xie* (Chinese spelling lists) along with him to Tasmania. He freely chose to pack the lists.

2 or 3 times during our 10-day stay in Tasmania, I asked him if he would like to learn some *ting xie* or play all day. Each time, he thought seriously about it, and then said no.

Each time, I shrugged my shoulders and hugged him, saying, "That is fine. You think about it and make a wise choice in view of the kind of results you are aiming for, and the other opportunities to catch up on your studies."

It was clear to him that I respected his choice. The whole idea was to let Little Boy experience a real choice when it comes to work, and play. I leveraged upon an occasion where it didn't matter whether he chose work or play, and I used it to signal to Little Boy that I gave him true choices.

This builds emotional and trust capital that I can use later on in the year when I really need him to work very hard. Later in the year, I constrain choices to "Shall we do Science or Math practices this week? Or shall we do 1 Science practice and 1 Math practice on alternate days?"

In the anecdote above, I showed that parents should make use of every situation to provide work-play choices.

Even during occasions where parents don't expect any work to be done, broadly autonomous work-play choices can be offered just so as to signal to the child that the parent does truly accept the child's choice. Such work-play choices can be broadly autonomous because the stakes are low and the parent truly doesn't care either way.

But some readers might ask if the parent truly does not mind letting the child play, then why offer a choice to work or play in the first place. Just let the child play. Well, I do it because I never want to pass up any opportunity to convince my child that he can freely pick from the choices I provide without fear of my disapproval. This builds trust that can be used later on when the parent must impose goals or constrain choices.

HOW MANY SUMS TO DO?

After returning from Tasmania, we allocated the last week of December 2011 to Math. I set a bottom limit for Math practice, stipulating that Little Boy needed only to complete 2 problem sums per sub-chapter of the assessment book. However, if he decided he needed practice, he could choose to do more.

He did indeed choose to do more for some sub-chapters to be very sure to master the topic. When I observed this, I widened his autonomy further because it was clear to me that he had developed some judgment about when to do more work, and when to do less. I let him know that I didn't mind even if he chose to skip some chapters if he thought these chapters not useful for exams.

I could afford to let Little Boy have so much autonomy because through Primary 3 and Primary 4, I had developed in him a strong feeling about the importance of consistent practice. I had also got him addicted to the joy of achieving. He wasn't about to short-change himself because he knew that if he skived here, he would deny himself the joy of goal achievement.

To learn how to get your child to this stage, you will need to start by giving constrained choices regularly (to stimulate cognitive dissonance, and further develop the mind to believe in the importance of and the fun of achieving in school). However, giving choices alone is not enough. You need to use the "giving structured choices" strategy in concert with the other strategies that you will slowly discover as you read through this book.

In the anecdote above, I want to show that broadly autonomous choices can also be offered when the child has already developed some wisdom in choice-making.

HOW TO PROVIDE STRUCTURED CHOICES

1. *The age of a child matters when you are structuring choices.* Choices for lower primary children should be well-defined and perhaps not as numerous. Choices for upper primary children can be less constrained. For example, when he was in Primary 2 (eight years old), I asked Little Boy to choose between doing his homework before his bath, or after. Later, when he was in Primary 4 (ten years old), I gave him three stacks of past year exam papers (one stack each for English, Mathematics and Science). I then asked him to plan on a weekly basis his own schedule for doing one paper from each subject stack. The choices given to The

Daughter when it comes to her schoolwork are even more loosely structured. For example, I leave it completely up to her to choose what to revise, how to revise and when to do it.

2. *The prior training of the child in choice-making also matters when you are structuring choices.* Unless you have started early on to expose your child to structured choices, you may not want to suddenly allow your older child (maybe Primary 5, or eleven years old) to start planning his own schedule. You may want to sit down on a weekly basis and plan it together for about three months before you allow the child to plan it himself. Without prior training in choice making, you may not even be able to leave your fifteen-year-old to structure his own revision schedule without some guidance.

3. *Be patient with your child.* Children don't develop judgment in a single day. It is you who will help them choose by providing a range of structure from the very well-defined (i.e., "Choose this, or that.") to the very undefined (i.e., "I leave it all up to you").

4. *When structuring loosely defined choices, it is important to set ground rules.* For example, the ground

SUN	MON	TUE	WED	THU	FRI	SAT
1 PLAY	2 OFF 5 MATH (P2)	3 ENG (P2)	4 ✳ SCI (P1)	5 CCA CHI (P2)	6 ENG COMPO	7 CHI COMPO SCI research
8 PLAY	9 OFF 5 MATH (P2)	10 BUFFET! MATH (P2)	11 ✳ MATH (P2)	(12) CCA CHI (P2)	13 ENG COMPO	14 CHI COMPO SCI research
15 (PLAY)	16 OFF 5 MATH (P1,P2)	17 CHI COMPO	18 ✳ SCI (P1) CHI COMPO	19 CCA CHI COMPO	(20) SCI (P2) CHI COMPO HOLIDAY!	21 PLAY J's bday party
22 CHI COMPO SCI research	(23) OFF 5 MATH (P2)	(24) ENG (P2)	25 SCI (P1,P2)	26 CCA CHI (P2)	27 (ENG COMPO)	28 CHI COMPO SCI research
29 PLAY SENTOSA!	30 OFF 5 (CHI (P1,P2))	31 MATH (P2)	REMEMBER: – clean my room – Mother's Day present			

rule for Little Boy when choosing books was "No baby books." The ground rule for Little Boy when planning his work schedule was "Complete one exam paper from each of the three stacks each week".

5. *It is important to check the child's choices especially when loosely defined choices have been given.* For example, I would review Little Boy's weekly work plan, and give some suggestions if I thought that he had planned too much or too little in one day.

6. *Be supportive of the choice your child has made.* Praise the wisdom of that choice. For example, when Little Boy planned his English exam practice for Wednesdays, I nodded and said "This is good. You come home late on Wednesdays and so it is wise to put the English paper here because you find English exams fastest to complete." Or, when Little Boy chose to do his homework after his bath, I said "That is good. You will feel refreshed and more energetic." If he had chosen to do his homework before his bath, I would have said "That is good. You will finish it earlier."

7. *Be sincere in offering the child choices.* Let him know that the choices made available are all choices you can live with, and that he is free to choose between them.

Don't provide a false choice in your selection and then manipulate the child's decision.

Emotional Connection

Inspired by the work of Professor Edward L. Deci and Professor Richard M. Ryan.

WHAT IS EMOTIONAL CONNECTION?

When the child is in the womb, he receives nourishment through the umbilical cord. The foetus' blood passes through the umbilical cord and gets detoxified by the Mother's liver and kidneys before passing back into the foetus. The mother nourishes the child physically. The mother's liver and kidneys are also responsible for removing toxic waste produced by normal metabolism.

Few people realise that nature intended for an emotional umbilical cord to link child to mother all through childhood. This is an invisible but very real link between you and your child. This virtual umbilical cord if strong and unblocked, transports emotional energy from you to your child. It also allows you to reach into the child's emotional reality to give emotional strength and remove toxic emotions. Through this emotional umbilical cord, you are attuned to your child's feelings. You sense and respond to his joys. You reach out through this connection to give comfort in his sadness. It is also this emotional umbilical cord that helps you feel what your child is feeling.

When my children are sad or hurt, I feel it keenly, to the extent that I find it hard to forgive those who were responsible for having hurt them before. If you do not share with your children this sense of emotional empathy, then it is important to fix this first before all else. With the help of your emotional connection, emotional energy can flow from you to your child when he is frightened and discouraged. He can then use your energy to cope with school challenges. In the face of the most daunting challenges to give up and go play, it will be the energy you feed to your child that will keep him on task... and committed to the goal he chose.

Unlike the physical umbilical cord which is exclusive to Mothers. Fathers can also build a strong emotional umbilical cord to the child. If neither Father nor Mother has this bond, then it can be Grandpa or Grandma... or some other adult who is a constant and long-term presence for the child. It is even better if the child can have a whole family of people to draw emotional sustenance from.

WHY MAINTAIN AN EMOTIONAL CONNECTION?

The Daughter once commented to Little Boy, "Bro, it never ends. When you learn to do something well and are happy about it, they will give you some thing else to do, that is depressingly difficult." In other words, school isn't easy. It isn't designed to be easy because school is there to teach you what you don't know. And what you don't know, is difficult. When things are difficult, many children will feel discouraged and give up. A child who has given up, will sit there and only do schoolwork when absolutely forced to.

Children need to be able to draw upon someone else's emotional energy in order to stay the course. They need emotional encouragement so that they don't run out of emotional energy, become discouraged and run out of motivation. Whose emotional energy should my child draw on, if not mine? If the child and the parent have a strong emotional connection, it makes it easier for the child to draw on the parent's emotional resources in order to keep striving at school. If your child is a natural genius,

then he may not need all this to do well. But we aren't a
family of geniuses, so we need all the help we can get to
maximise our performance.

WHY IS EMOTIONAL CONNECTION IMPORTANT?

Emotional connection between people is a powerful
motivating force. How so?

I recently completed a research study in a high-tech
manufacturing organisation where old-timers shrug like
cowboys and drawl with understated arrogance, "Ma'am,
if it's an impossible goal, that's the right one to set". It is a
most endearing organisation filled with down-to-earth and
serious-minded engineer cowboys. I close my eyes and can
almost see their CEO sitting lazily on a horse, with a
cigarette butt hanging from the corner of his mouth lazily
drawling "Yeah... Impossible goals. I've been there and
done that. Yeah..."

I interviewed people in that organisation asking them
to tell me about a work goal they had previously attained
which was so very challenging that they had almost given
up, but they didn't. These people told me stories that made
me cry after the interviews. Some people stepped into the
interview, began crying after 20 minutes and didn't stop

crying until they stepped out. That was how hellish some of their experiences had been.

One lady was asked to develop a test for a random production error that would likely occur only once every 20 years, but whose occurrence spelt disaster in epic proportions. At one point, the challenges of the task were so great that she woke up every hour in the night. "One o'clock. Two o'clock. 3 a.m. I cannot sleep. 4 a.m. I keep thinking if I should throw in the towel, go in tomorrow and tell my boss 'That's it! I'm leaving!'" Yet, she didn't leave. She credited her boss and her boss' boss for providing the understanding, the help and the emotional support she needed to stay committed to a task that she was convinced was way beyond her capability. Her spouse too played a very large part. Her spouse said "Quit if you want to. I'm sure we'll manage!" Right in the middle of the interview, my head jerked back and I blinked a few times. I thought it was really odd. Hey, if your goal was impossible, and your spouse supported your resignation from the organisation, why didn't you quit? It didn't make sense!

Now, I realise that it was the unconditional acceptance from her spouse that came through a very strong emotional connection between husband and wife, through which the lady engineer drew energy and encouragement to finally achieve the impossible. If you want your children to achieve very difficult things, you must be there for them. Since school is difficult by definition, you must be there to encourage them through the hell and high water of school exams and school homework. The emotional connection between parent and child must have the bandwidth of fibre optic cable, not the bandwidth of Internet dial-up. The following family anecdote illustrates the power of emotional connection.

4-DIGIT LONG DIVISION

When Little Boy completed his Primary 2 end-of-year exams, it seemed appropriate for me to invest in Andrew Er's Mathematics Worksheets for Primary 3, and get him to do the odd sum over the December holidays. Little Boy chose to do four problem sums every weekday from the book.

What I hadn't accounted for was that those sums were REALLY difficult. When he got to question 19 on page 22 of the assessment book, I realised that he needed to know 4-digit long division. Even then, I didn't realise how difficult 4-digit long division actually was for a little boy who had just only completed Primary 2! If you search the Internet for the Singapore Ministry of Education's Mathematics Syllabus, you will read that 4-digit long division is planned for Primary 4. I didn't know that until too late because I was following the Primary 2 assessment book without realising that it was setting questions from the Primary 4 syllabus.

As a result of my own incompetence as a Math teacher, I had structured choices for Little Boy that were way beyond his ability level. I had asked him to choose 3, 4 or 5 problem sums to do every weekday, from Andrew Er's Mathematics Worksheets. He chose 4. Of course, when he got to page 22, he was so frustrated that he was almost in tears.

I took him in my arms and explained that it was ok to not know. After all, this was Primary 4 work and since he was only a

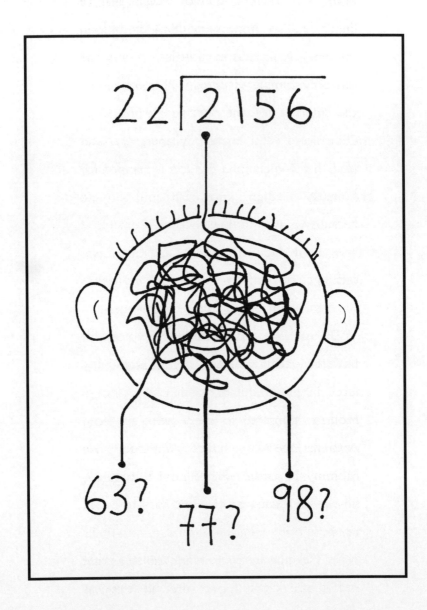

Primary 2, there was every reason not to know. But I reckoned that it was an imminently teachable moment. It was the golden moment to teach my son that he could do things that looked impossible.

I slowly went through 5 different 4-digit long division sums with him. He plodded through another 15 slowly and with great difficulty. Yet, he persisted. And I'll tell you why. Partly, it was because he had initially chosen to complete the 20 long division sums. Mostly though, it was because of my nose.

Mother and son, we have a joke between us that Mommy has a magic nose. Every time Little Boy gets frustrated with his work, all Mommy needs to do, is to stick her nose onto his cheek and energy will flow from Mommy to Little Boy. Of course it sounds silly. It's supposed to. But the moment I stick my nose onto his cheek, his frustration melts away. He giggles. The problem is still there and is still difficult, but his frustration is lessened, and he renews his focus on the problem. What my nose provides is not the solution to the problem, but enough emotional comfort to keep him going, and I keep topping up until he reaches the end.

I stuck my nose onto his cheek and told him that even if he knew nothing at all, I would still love him. I told him that even if he got every sum wrong, I would still love him. One by one, he tackled each sum. If he got one right, I praised him. If he got one wrong, I gently rubbed the working away and went through the sum again step by step. Every now and then, I stuck my nose onto his cheek for a few seconds. One sum at a time, he got them done. It took him 4 hours of very painful effort.

At the end of the day, Little Boy was so proud of having done what he had thought to be impossible. He was exuberant and gambolled around the house like a puppy. He almost fell down the stairs in his hurry to meet his father at the door and he crowed his triumph whilst jumping up and down. There was an amazing amount of energy.

And guess what! The next morning, I gave him a choice: four easy problem sums, or another 20 long division sums. I proposed four easy problem sums because I thought to give him an easy day after the previously gruelling one. My brave Little Boy chose 20 long division sums. He said, "It's more difficult and therefore, more fun!!"

It seemed to me that he wanted to recapture the rush of ecstatic joy that came from achieving what he thought to be impossible. He was clearly beginning to enjoy the process of doing schoolwork. That is very high internal drive. To want to do something for the sheer enjoyment of it, is Level 3 internal drive.

THE CHALLENGES OF MAINTAINING AN EMOTIONAL CONNECTION

Challenge 4.1:   *Parental Fear*

Parents may be afraid. I know that I sometimes am. We're afraid that the child will do poorly, lose out academically, and later, lose out in life. In our fear, we lash out at our children. We get angry and we say hurtful things such as "You're stupid and lazy." Even if we don't say hurtful things, our tone of voice and body language communicate displeasure and disapproval. Our children become sad. Sadness is an emotional state that is characterised by a lack of emotional energy. You won't have energy for school if you are feeling sad about school work. In order to spare Little Boy the edge of my own frustration, I often have to remind myself that many adults, who plodded along as students, have found success in life. This way, I don't get too fixated on school results, but I focus on my child instead.

Challenge 4.2:   *Parental Pride and Stress*

Parents may identify too much with their children's school performance. Parents may feel ashamed when their children do not perform well. These unpleasant emotions interfere with the parent's ability to offer emotional encouragement. I often have to remind myself that if my child does poorly in school, I should be less attuned to my own emotional state, and more attuned to his. Ashamed or not, the child is still mine, and if we have to share the shame together, so be it. I would rather be ashamed than see my child unhappy.

Parents can also be stressed by other things and barely have enough emotional resources to cope with their own stress, leaving none for the child to draw upon.

Challenge 4.3:   *Parents' Own Sense of Incompetence*

Parents can get angry when trying to help our children, not because there is anything wrong with them, but because we ourselves feel helpless and inadequate. The next family anecdote illustrates how easy it is for parents to weaken the emotional connection with our children when we ourselves feel incompetent at teaching them, and the immediate negative consequences of the weakened link.

THE MOON DOES NOT BLOCK THE SUN

Little Boy could not figure out the relative orbits of the moon, the sun and the earth. It was confusing for me too. I knew that everything turned on its axis, and that everything turned around each other but I couldn't explain it properly. I was also feeling anxious because I had a stack of my own students' exams to mark and our helper had just burnt our dinner in the wok. And I was tired.

All my negativity was barely held in check as I tried to explain to Little Boy why the moon does not block the sun during the new moon phase. I didn't even know what a new moon was! I found a YouTube video and asked Little Boy to sit down and view it. I thought the video was quite clear. But Little Boy still couldn't understand why during the new moon phase, the moon does not block out the sun.

Barely able to control my temper, I set up an exhibit with a wall (representing the sun), a basketball (representing the moon) and Little Boy (representing the earth) and I sputtered myself silly as I pushed Little Boy here and there (none too gently). Once or twice he paused to think with his mouth wide open. I wanted to scream "Hurry up! Why can't you get it? You must be stupid!" But luckily, I didn't.

Even then, the more I sputtered, the wider went Little Boy's eyes. I asked "Do you get it?" a few times. Each time I asked it louder. The first time I asked the question, Little Boy said "I almost get it." The fourth time I asked the question, Little Boy's face was contorted in an expression of fearful frustration, and he said "I don't get it at all." I didn't verbally call him stupid, but all my gestures and my tone of voice were beginning to make him think he was stupid.

I took a deep breath and calmed myself down. Then I said, "No, no. You have almost got it. This is difficult because everything turns around everything. The earth turns. The moon turns. The sun turns (I think). And they all dance around each other!! Even I don't understand!" Then we danced around the wall, the basketball and Little Boy a while more and then, Little Boy understood.

That evening, around the dining table, The Husband asked the same question that Little Boy did earlier (see, I told you primary school in Singapore isn't easy). I sputtered again, trying to explain. Little Boy stood up and did an excellent explanation without sputtering.

As you can see from the above anecdote, my anger and frustration prevented me from topping up Little Boy's stores of emotional energy. I was so busy using up my own emotional energy to feed my frustration that he could draw no clean energy from me. He was drawing energy poisoned with anger and frustration. I could feel Little Boy's emotional strength wilting, and with insufficient emotional energy, he couldn't move his own understanding of the difficult material forwards.

It's the difference between refreshing yourself with clean and pure spring water, or water tainted with bacteria or petrol. The effects can be immediately felt. Drinking clean spring water gives you physical strength to carry on. Drinking tainted spring water can make you feel ill and weak. However, when I calmed down and made a conscious effort to give him emotional encouragement, Little Boy figured out his conundrum soon after.

HOW TO MAINTAIN AN EMOTIONAL CONNECTION

1. In order to strengthen the emotional connection, it helps to *make your child feel that if ever you could choose to buy any child at all from a selection of children at the supermarket, you would definitely buy him over and over again, and no one else.* This communicates unconditional love and acceptance.

2. *Being aware of your own feelings is important.* If you are aware of your own feelings and their origins, you can better control them. Feelings are contagious. If your heart is full of anger and frustration, your child draws upon harmful negative emotional energy. If this happens too much, the child's instinct for self-preservation will kick in. He will try to withdraw from you emotionally. This will shrink the emotional umbilical cord between parent and child, so necessary to feed the child with emotional resources. In the worst case, it may completely shrivel up into nothing. This leaves your child alone to face the many challenges posed by school. He will be lonely, fearful and miserable. Far in the future, it may leave you emotionally alone to face the many challenges of old age. Just as emotional energy can flow from you to your

child at a time when he is weak, the energy can also flow through the same emotional connection, from your child to you when you are old and weak. Pregnant women try not to feed themselves potentially toxic food such as alcohol and strong medicines because they are aware they can poison the growing foetus in the womb. Adults who are linked emotionally to any child should realise that unless they are careful, they could be poisoning their children's emotional health too.

3. The emotional umbilical cord is a given in any loving relationship. A child's trust and loyalty is yours to lose. *The emotional umbilical cord is yours to destroy.* Parents don't have to make special effort to build an emotional connection. You just have to take what nature gave, maintain it and make it stronger.

4. *Telling yourself that your child matters more to you than school results, helps.* After all, many adults have found success in life despite being very average students. Once one is able to do this, it can become much easier to calm ourselves down enough to encourage our child out of his rut of poor performance. Anger and frustration will only discourage your child into staying inside that rut of poor performance. The

irony is that the more you tell yourself this, the easier it is for you to give your child clean and pure emotional energy. Your child can then use this extra emotional energy to stay engaged. Eventually, your child will do much better than you ever imagined.

5. *It helps to try and imagine yourself in the place of your child.* Be sensitive to the child's facial expressions and body language. This helps you to be attuned to the child's emotional state, and when you do that, it becomes easier to ignore your own emotional state. Being attuned strengthens the emotional umbilical cord.

6. *Make a conscious effort to be encouraging.*

7. *Focus more on the process that leads to success,* than on results. The following chapter will expand on this.

8. *Leave it till another day* if you are tired out from work or suffering from a headache.

5 Focus on Study Process, Not Grades

Inspired by the work of Professor Richard Lazarus and Professor Susan Folkman.

WHAT IS STUDY PROCESS?

A study process is a sequence of study activities, habits or behaviours developed collaboratively by you and your child. Each specific behaviour in the sequence of behaviours is clearly defined. The process defines even the study materials used by the child. See an example of a study process below.

Learning Stage (From 5 up to 2 months before exams)

1	Read through one topic in the Science textbook.
2	Locate the same topic in the Science Booster Volumes.
3	Whilst reading the material in the Science Booster Volumes, use little Post-Its to flag out the details that Little Boy is curious to know more about.

4	Go on the Internet and research more about these details. Use the relevant key words and the words "Kids' Science" when searching.

Exam Preparation Stage (From 2 months before exams)

1	Do 1 practice exam from 2010 every week.
2	Mark the practice exam using the answer sheet given.
3	Flag out with Post-It stickers the questions he did not know.
4	Do further Internet research or ask his Science Teacher for help with the difficult questions.

Figure 5.1   Study Process: Learning and Exam Preparation

There are as many study processes as there are students and teachers and subjects. Over the years, I have had to refine and change Little Boy's study processes again and again, in response to changes in his situation. The child's study process needs to be tailored to his situation, his age, and changed when he changes or ages, or when the situation changes. Little Boy's very first study process was very simple. He was only three years old.

1	Go and pee.
2	Play any Dr Seuss computer game two times. Do not get up until after you are done.

Figure 5.2   Little Boy's Very First Study Process

WHY IS IT IMPORTANT TO FOCUS ON PROCESS?

Reason 5.1: The Jack Welch Model of Performance Management

Many years ago, Jack Welch, the then CEO of General Electric made popular a notion that I adapted for my kids. Jack Welch apparently advocated that managers who could deliver excellent results without doing it the accepted GE way needed to be counselled or even fired (see Quadrant 2 below). This was because excellent results can be achieved in harmful ways i.e., over-aggressive selling techniques etc... which would then come back to haunt GE in the future. These are behaviours that bring excellent results, but they are wrong behaviours. Such managers, said Jack Welch, could deliver excellent results only in the short term. In the long term, their results will slowly degrade.

	Weak Process	Robust Process
Excellent Results	Quadrant 2 Fire or counsel the employee.	Quadrant 3 Reward the employee.
Poor Results	Quadrant 1 Fire the employee.	Quadrant 4 Be patient with the employee.

Figure 5.3   Jack Welch's Model of Employee Management

Conversely, Jack Welch advocated being patient with managers who were demonstrating all the correct behaviours at work but were not yet delivering results (see Quadrant 4 in Figure 5.3 above). Since all the right behaviours for success were being demonstrated, success would not be far off. One just needed to be patient.

This was advice I took to heart as a parent. I began to focus more on the study process (i.e., behaviours that would lead to success), and less on results (i.e., grades). However, I adapted Jack Welch's notion a little, because whilst one can fire employees, one cannot fire one's own children.

Primary 1 and Primary 2 are the least challenging years of the child's entire school career. Most parents know that in these two years, it is possible to score well for tests if the parent is diligent in giving the child enough practice exercises, helps the child pack his bag, file his papers etc... However, such a study process is weak because all the effort is on the part of the parent, not the child (see Quadrant 2 of Figure 5.4 below). The child demonstrates none of the behaviours that lead to success. As such the excellent results achieved in Primary 1 and 2 with parental help is unsustainable through to Primary 6, unless the child is allowed to catch up on his behavioural training, and quickly masters the study behaviours that lead to academic success.

	Weak Process	Robust Process
Excellent Results	Quadrant 2 Don't wait! Review process now!	Quadrant 3 Celebrate!
Poor Results	Quadrant 1 There is still hope if you do process review!	Quadrant 4 Encourage the child.

Figure 5.4   Adapted Model of Student Management

Of course, if in Primary 1 & 2, your child can deliver on both process and results, there is nothing to worry about (see Quadrant 3 above). It is cause for celebration because you're off to a good start. However, my kids weren't able to deliver on both process and results in lower primary. As such I chose to focus more on process and less on results, because I believed that if my children could master process, then sustainable results would follow (see Quadrant 4 above).

Reason 5.2:   *Process Focus Motivates*

However, I had another reason to focus more on process, than results. Focusing on process motivates. Here is why. When a parent focuses on grades, the child too will focus on grades. A child who focuses on grades risks frequent disappointments because only one person can top the class at any one time. Or, only 10 people can get into the top 10 positions at any one time. This means that the majority of our children will be disappointed. A child who feels like a loser in school won't be motivated to work hard at school.

When a parent focuses on process, the child too will focus on process. A child who focuses on process is buffered from the competitiveness of the school system. Process development is a rewarding journey because you compete against yourself only; and with practice, you do better than the past and win against yourself. One feels a sense of progression when focusing on process because process skills get better with practice. The sense of making progress is motivating in itself. For example, the first time Little Boy sat down to play the Dr Seuss' Alphabet computer games, he could only manage two games. Gradually, he progressed to three, four, five and then six games. Compared to what he could do previously,

completing five games was better than the four earlier, than the three even earlier and than the two at the start. I made such a big fuss about him completing more and more games that Little Boy felt proud and happy. He felt that he had achieved something by completing up to six games (the maximum I required). With this as a daily process, the more games he played, the better scores he achieved, and before we both realised, he had learnt his ABCs, without me having to evaluate his results in too obvious a manner.

Reason 5.3: Process Focus Builds Resilience to Disappointment

Next, a child who has been focusing attention on, and practicing process skills (i.e., the behaviours that lead to academic success) is more resilient when faced with poorer than hoped for results. When he looks at his poor grades, he does not feel helpless. He will learn to reflect on his study process and troubleshoot it for better results. A child who focuses on process skills learns to tweak his study process when his grades are poor. He learns to change his behaviours to get different results.

Students who focus on process tend not to be blindsided by disempowering thoughts such as "I am stupid and it can't be helped". Parents who focus on process tend not to be blindsided by thoughts such as "My child is not bright so let's not expect too much". Both parent and child are willing to keep on trying because there is always possibility of improving the process. There is never such a thing as the perfect process. When children and parent know that something specific can be changed in the study process in order to get better results, they begin to hope again. Hope motivates (see Quadrant 1 of Figure 5.4 above).

Knowing specifically that something can be done about process is more motivating than not knowing what to do at all when one receives a poor grade. Of course, adults will always say "Work harder" but that is a very vague prescription. How exactly can one work? Some children, who have already been working very hard, but not effectively, may decide to completely not care about school altogether when they get bad grades. Simply, they have no idea how to improve their grades. They lose hope. They crumble. Focusing on process gives hope because it provides a possible solution to poor grades. In the following family anecdote, I will share how focusing on process helps the child stay resilient in the face of disappointment, and motivates the child to be persistent. It also shows how persistence translates naturally into better results.

Scoring Poorly for Chinese

At the end of Primary 4 in December 2010, Little Boy had scored more than 90% for Math, Science and English. For Chinese, he had scored only 79%. This was a disappointing grade because he had worked very hard. Every week for months before the exams, he had memorised five Chinese proverbs, completed one practice Chinese exam paper, and written one Chinese composition. That was our process.

All this work was over and above the deluge of Chinese homework he had had to cope with from his Chinese Teacher. We completely neglected English practices so that he would have time for Chinese. We even halved the numbers of Science Practices to be done so as to give Chinese more time. Yet, he scored far worse for Chinese than for the other subjects. He was very disappointed indeed. It was a demoralising moment even for me.

So I said to him, "I'm not upset that you scored poorly for Chinese. I saw how diligent you were in doing all you were supposed to do. I am very proud of you because you behaved like a Boy of Character. Too bad you did poorly. But there is hope. Maybe there is something wrong with the way you were studying? Let's see if we can improve the process of studying."

One little girl in Little Boy's class had scored full marks for her Chinese composition exam. Little Boy was sent back to school to suss out the little girl's study process. His little lady friend was generous in her sharing. She said "I memorise tons of model Chinese essays."

A light bulb went on in my head. Aaaah! So that's how one aces Chinese. I packed the whole family off to Beijing, got hold of 4 volumes of 1000 model Chinese essays (a collection of the best from China's PSLE equivalent). The essays were difficult. The Daughter thought that even secondary school students might have trouble reading them.

Grandma helped by reading the essays into a digital recorder stored in Little Boy's laptop. We soon developed a process wherein…

1	Grandma highlighted and explained the unfamiliar words.
2	Little Boy divided the essay into small chunks of three sentences each with his pencil.
3	He would listen to the recording, and memorise each chunk by both reading aloud and listening.
4	Once he had mastered each chunk, he would come and look for me, or call me on the phone to recite it to me (before he forgot it again).

Figure 5.5   Study Process: Chinese

Being able to recite each small part to me allowed him to feel a sense of achievement. These small milestones gave him small infusions of motivational energy. These kept him going till the end of each difficult essay. At the end of the day, he could read the essay to me fluently.

And he felt good.

In the beginning, it was tough. He could only memorise three sentences at a time. A single essay required six hours to properly memorise. For me too, it was tough. I needed to make myself available whenever he was ready to recite his few sentences.

However, by doing things vastly differently, we began to get vastly different results. Before we knew it, he was scoring better marks at his *ting xie* and Chinese comprehension. He even scored very well for oral simply because he could recognise more words and could read the oral passage confidently and with a depth of expression. In fact, he scored better for Chinese Oral than his English Oral in Primary 5!

THE CHALLENGES OF FOCUSING ON PROCESS

Challenge 5.1:   *Controlling Your Emotional State*

Focusing on process is one of the most difficult things to do. When a child's grades are poor, parents cannot help their own emotional response. When something valuable is broken, it is human nature to sit down and mourn over the broken shards, like they were broken dreams. If you imagine that every exam paper is a Ming Dynasty vase, then every time the child receives a poor grade, you will feel a devastating sense of loss. With this devastating sense of loss weighing upon your heart, it is hard to look beyond the broken debris of unrealised hopes. Instead, it may help to view certain exams as fake Ming Dynasty vases only, to be used for practice. When the replica Ming Dynasty vase is broken, it is easier to discount it and focus on discussing how the process of carrying that vase from one place to another can be improved.

For Little Boy, the really important exams were in Primary 2, Primary 4 and Primary 6. Children were streamed into ability bands at the end of Primary 2. This would happen again in Primary 4. In Primary 6, there was the all-important PSLE. I paid special attention to mid-year and end-year exams in these 3 years. In Primary 2, I helped Little Boy enough to ensure that he went into a good class. He didn't have to top the class, but I didn't want him to end up in a poor class with disruptive students. Apart from these more important exams, all other exams were occasions where I allowed Little Boy to try and manage his

study process more or less independently, with predictably, less than ideal exam scores.

In other words, when I deemed an exam as less important, I allowed Little Boy to try carrying it himself. This not only gave him enough opportunity to practice managing his study processes independently, it also allowed him to experience first hand, the consequences of poor process skills (e.g., lack of diligence and discipline). For example, when he did not do well in Primary 3, he learnt to feel the importance of diligence and discipline.

In Primary 3, Little Boy ranked 28th in a class of 38 pupils. Nonetheless, I considered that we had achieved a lot in Primary 3. In that year, Little Boy fine-tuned the independent study processes that had carried his sister through from PSLE through to 8 distinctions at the 'A' levels. I consciously refrained from reminding him. We worked out task lists and schedules and if he didn't do them as we had agreed, his grades suffered. When his report book came back, I looked past the grades and gave him very specific feedback about his study process, e.g.,

If you think you still don't understand a certain math topic, then you can search for explanations on the Internet.

⚲ You were not consistent enough because you didn't complete one math practice a week like we had discussed.

⚲ If you don't practice enough, there is no way to be fast in your calculations.

In Primary 4, armed with the process skills mastered in Primary 3 (and a deep feeling that such process skills are important), Little Boy ended the year 8th in a class of 38.

Challenge 5.2:   *Not Easy to Troubleshoot Process*

Another difficulty when focusing on process is in knowing how to design process. What are the behaviours that lead to success? The wrong process design will use up your child's effort and energy without leading to good results. This can be demotivating. In the following family anecdote, I will share with you how we got our process design for learning Chinese wrong, not once, but twice.

LEARNING CHINESE: INEFFECTIVE PROCESS 1

Grandma taught Little Boy Chinese from a whole stack of assessment books. Every week, she was diligent in drilling Little Boy in his *ting xie*. She handwrote stacks and stacks of

81

memory cards and expected him to memorise words, expressions and their pronunciations. Even then, I had my reservations about this study process but I could not put a finger on what made me uncomfortable. I let things drift along and Little Boy's Chinese grades dropped steadily.

Later, I realised that Grandma's method required a Chinese-speaking environment in the home. Every memory card took words and expressions out of context. This is fine for a child who speaks Chinese at home because he would have absorbed many word usages in daily life. Such a child would only need to memorise the characters and their pronunciations to become literate. The study process ignored the fact that Little Boy had little idea what the words on the memory cards meant in context. Not knowing what they meant, he couldn't use them, and found it doubly hard to remember them. Making him memorise expressions on cards took a lot of his time and added little to his competence in the language. And it was so boring to memorise lists and lists of disembodied words.

You see, Little Boy is a Potato Kid (i.e. a child who speaks English at home). He shouldn't be learning Chinese the way Rice Kids (i.e. children who speak Chinese at home) do.

LEARNING CHINESE: INEFFECTIVE PROCESS 2

When Little Boy came to the end of Primary 3, it was clear that Grandma's process didn't work. What was wrong? I really scratched my head. I am illiterate in Chinese and Grandma was absolutely certain that her study process was perfect, and if the grades were heading south, it was because (1) Little Boy just wasn't smart enough, (2) Little Boy just wasn't hardworking enough, (3) Little Boy's mother's (me!) deep prejudice against all things Chinese had created a mental block in him, or (4) Little Boy was simply born that way. I pooh-poohed these ideas because I was convinced that if we could find the right process, we would be able to get better results.

I refused to believe that Little Boy was stupid (after all, he was scoring well for other subjects). I knew he wasn't lazy because I saw the hours and the effort he put in. No way was I going to admit that I was prejudiced against all things Chinese! Hmmmmmph! And what's this about being born that way? If Malay students can score A1 in Chinese, then how come Little Boy was born not being able to learn Chinese? We are Chinese, aren't we? What would have happened if Little Boy were born in China? Would it mean that if he were born in China, he would never learn to communicate simply because he was born not being able to get Chinese? Not being able to get Chinese is some sort of genetic disease? What nonsense!

So I tweaked Little Boy's Chinese study process. I made Little Boy memorise a Chinese proverb everyday because I had read in the newspapers that a very successful Singaporean advertising executive who made millions in

China from her language skills, had memorised reams of Chinese proverbs when she was little. Oh well... this didn't work either. It was very frustrating! What was wrong with our process?

I later realised that I too was making him memorise Chinese proverbs outside of context. Poor Little Boy! He was so sweet and patient with me, and he trusted me so completely! But I didn't know what was wrong with his study process.

LEARNING CHINESE: FINALLY, AN EFFECTIVE PROCESS

We finally found an effective process when Little Boy settled into memorising and reciting highly challenging Chinese model compositions written by 12-year-olds in China. Little Boy recited each model Chinese composition to me in portions and ended off by reading me the whole text fluently, and with expression. He also taught me the meanings of the words I didn't understand.

He immersed himself in the Chinese text in context. From this unnatural immersion, he absorbed words, their usage and their meanings.

He was later able to suggest a process enhancement. He told me that he wished to take a break from memorising the text in order to (1) highlight the words that could come in useful in writing compositions, (2) copy them out so that he could learn to write them. I was thrilled. He had heard and seen many new words in context. He understood what they meant, how they were pronounced, how they were used, and he naturally felt compelled to learn to write them, in order that he could complete his learning.

You see, I had focused on process (refusing to accept that he was incapable of learning Chinese), and thus Little Boy learnt to look at process too (without thinking himself genetically incapable of learning Chinese). The moment one acknowledges "I cannot do it because I am genetically

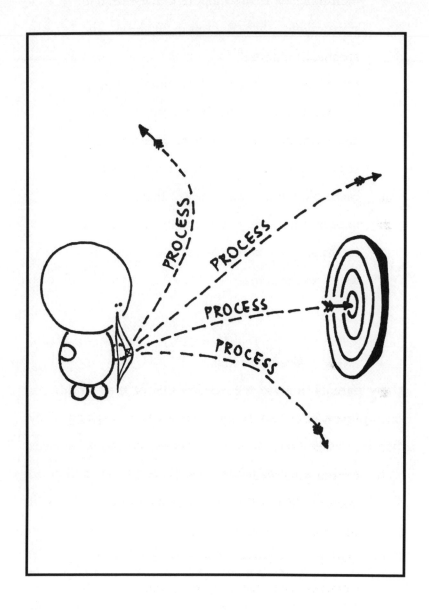

incapable", one will stop trying. Once one stops trying, then it cannot be done. The prophecy fulfils itself.

Figuring out a good process isn't easy, but focusing on process means that we won't give up hope. It took us many years to figure out a process that worked, but hope kept us going because we knew that process improvements are always possible and that if we found the right process, we would get better results.[†]

Challenge 5.3: Realising That More Of The Same Won't Make A Difference To Results

Many parents analyse the weaknesses of their children's exam papers, and then isolate weak areas to work on. They then buy assessment book after assessment book to focus on these weak areas *ad nauseum*. If the results are still poor, they look for another better and newer assessment book. It

---

[†] I have, in the past, documented for free access the psychological underpinnings of Potato Chinese™. I will not repeat this here. Parents interested in knowing more about teaching Potato Kids Chinese can log on to http://petunialee.blogspot.sg/2011/10/learning-chinese-potato-wa y.html.

A Side Note: Use Of Assessment Books

I am not saying that assessment books don't help at all. They are effective drilling tools i.e., they serve to reinforce what has been learnt. They are good for practice. However, before one begins to drill and practice, one must first learn. In my opinion, assessment books are not effective learning tools.

Take our case as an example. It was clear that Chinese assessment books did not work. On hindsight, we now know that assessments provide practices, drills and evaluations. They don't help you learn.

Learning needs to take place before evaluation and we hit the jackpot when we exposed Little Boy to many new Chinese words everyday by getting him to memorise and recite. This was very intense learning.

For years, we had relied on Chinese assessment books to LEARN with. This was very ineffective for learning Chinese because Little Boy got stuck at every second question. And the only learning to be had was through every mistake. This was hardly motivating because every mistake served to signal to Little Boy that he was dumb. No wonder he hated Chinese!!

Getting Little Boy to memorise and recite high volumes of Chinese exposed him to a high volume of positive models of the language. He was learning without having to make mistakes. Only when he had learnt enough did we begin to drill him with assessment worksheets. We never forgot this lesson when designing study processes for Little Boy. Learning must precede drilling and practice.

would help to reconsider whether assessment books help at all in the whole study process. More of the same process will give you exactly the same results.

HOW TO FOCUS ON PROCESS?

1. *Break up a process into a sequence of separate and observable behaviours.* This allows you to clearly explain to your child what the behaviours are. When the child is little, there is no need to explain all the behaviours all at once. Focus on one until the child has mastered it. For example, for a long time, Little Boy thought the process of being diligent meant "sit at the desk to complete a short piece of work without getting up". Later, the process of being diligent was expanded to include "not watching TV". Still later, the process of being diligent was expanded to include "complete one past year math exam paper from Year 2009 every Thursday afternoon". Notice how specific each behavioural description is? It comprises even the specific resource material to be used.

2. *Check in on the child's enactment of these observable behaviours.* When introducing a new behaviour, I made sure that I checked in and reinforced the behaviour

every time. For example, when he was a toddler, I would sit with Little Boy to complete a short piece of work and once he had completed it without getting up, I praised him. This close monitoring does not last long. Once Little Boy had successfully enacted the behaviour I wanted a few times, I knew that he had understood what I wanted. Henceforth, I stopped checking in and reinforcing every time. Instead, I transited into a less frequent and more random monitoring and reinforcement schedule. I wandered in and out of the room. Or I went out for a meeting. Or I went and baked a cake. Once in a while, I would remember to check in. If I found him at his desk at work on the short piece of assignment, I praised him. If he was up and playing with his toys, he was scolded. This is a strategy called random intermittent variable reinforcement (RIVR) and will be described in greater detail in Chapter 7.

3. *Ensure that the behavioural steps are simple enough for the child to self-monitor.* For example, a parent I know insists that her child hop around from chapter to chapter in the assessment book. On Monday do Chapter 4. On Tuesday do Chapter 6. On Wednesday Chapter 2, and then Chapter 10. The parent wanted to

follow the sequence of chapters as taught by the school. The book was organised in a different sequence. This was confusing for the child who was lost without the needed daily instructions from his Mother. When I work with Little Boy, we will follow the sequence of the book so that Little Boy is fully aware of what his next steps are without having to check with me every day. I figured that eventually, both at school and at home we would have covered the same syllabus even if we didn't do it in the same sequence as the school. Knowing specifically what one needs to do without always having to check with a figure of authority is the first step to working independently. Hence, if you insist on hopping around the textbook, it would be good to list out the work schedule and place it up on the wall so that the child can independently refer to it.

4. *Develop a way to help your child self-monitor these observable behaviours.* This allows your child to control the process. This can be a simple checklist. Your child can be given a statement that reads "I finished Chapter 5 today without getting up to play"; and he gets to tick "Yes" or "No" next to the statement. If the child gets one short assignment every day of the week,

you can stick a single sheet of paper on his room door with 5 identical statements (one for each day of the week). He can then have the satisfaction of ticking each statement once he has enacted the required behaviour. Remember to celebrate successful enactment of the behaviour even though the results of the learning are still poor. People always start off bad at something so it is important to be happy about the behaviours that lead to success, even if success is nowhere in sight as yet.

5. *Initially, the child's self-monitoring can take place at the same time as your monitoring.* Slowly, you should phase yourself out of the monitoring process and leave your child to monitor. This is important because we are developing internal drive. To get your child to internalise a set of desired behaviours, he must be given ownership of them.

6. *Provide everything the child needs to enact the behaviour.* For example, if you want him to do step-by-step math practice, you must get ready a good quality step-by-step math assessment book with explanations.

7. *Be sure to include only very high quality materials into your process* because poor quality materials do not do justice to the time and effort your child will put into

implementing the process. Badly chosen assessment books tire your children and don't help them learn. Assessment practices done at the wrong point of the study process (i.e., before learning has taken place) are also a waste of time. If every minute of your child's time were $100, how would you spend that time?

8. *Once the behaviour is stable and acquired, there is usually no need to monitor nor reinforce anymore.* For example, once Little Boy had figured out that he could complete six Dr Seuss Alphabet games, he did it everyday by himself after breakfast before he went off to play the rest of the day. This started off as a set goal. It turned into an unspoken expectation, which later became a habit.

9. *Be very firm when the child is not diligent about his study process.* As long as I can see that my children are conscientious about the study process, I am happy to ignore poor grades. Once, Little Boy scored 54% for Chinese but I saw that he had worked very hard so I said "Oh well… at least you're not last in class. You're only 2nd last." However, if I notice that my child has not been managing himself properly, poor grades can become the trigger point for a hair-tearing explosion

that builds up into the Mother Medusa of rages focused on process diligence. Actually, whenever I see poor study process management, no grade is high enough. If they score 90, I want 100. But if I see diligent process management, I am happy with even 60 marks because I know that they tried their best, and asking for more would demoralise them.

10. *It is important to design the right process.* This requires the parent to evaluate the process often. I usually do it after every exam. The following may help parents evaluate their children's study processes.

   Are the materials used of excellent quality? This is important because a study process will use up the child's time and energy. Given the challenges of the Singapore education system, the child's time and energy are very scarce and precious resources. I had read through many of the English model compositions on sale in the local bookstores. They were grammatically correct and contained good vocabulary. But there was neither music nor poetry in the language used. I assumed that the collections of model Chinese compositions would be of similar mediocre quality. That was why I

A Side Note: Mother Medusa Tantrums

There is a time and a place for angry remonstrations in every parent's panoply of child-rearing tools. However, I try as far as possible to keep these few and far between. On average, I turn into Mama Medusa about once in 2 to 3 years. With Little Boy, it has been 2 years since the last metamorphosis.

If I must get angry, however, I make a memorable performance of it. Once I start, I work myself up into a real fury where my voice goes through every register of every scale. It even hits notes undetectable by the human ear. The performance typically lasts 2 hours at least. The performance is seared into the memory circuits of the guilty party. I do this for contrast. Since the normal me is loving and patient, the guilty one will go to great lengths to have the normal me back again. The same guilty one will go to great lengths to prevent the change over from Mother Theresa to Mother Medusa.

An established theory from stress research lies at the bottom of this strategy. It is called the conservation of resources theory[2]. This theory states that people are far keener to avoid loss, than they are to achieve gains. The thought of losing $10,000 will motivate you to action far better than the thought of gaining $10,000. In other words, people hate losing.

It is thus important to give your children something to lose. As far as I can, I smother my children with deep rich love. I make sure they revel in it. My children don't want to lose this precious resource. They go to great lengths NEVER to repeat a behaviour that was the cause of a Mother Medusa transformation. They go to great lengths to predict and avoid any behaviour that might lead to the next Mother Medusa transformation.

However, Mother Medusa transformations cannot be completely random. They need to be linked to a very specific undesirable behaviour. Else, children will feel very insecure about the parent's temper. Go easy on the Mother Medusa transformations with very young children. They are easily frightened so you don't need such a passionate performance.

chose to buy the model compositions produced by China's best students instead.

⚲ *Does your process distinguish between learning stage and drilling stage?* In the learning stage, Little Boy is allowed to refer to any sort of reference material available. When I asked him to do the math topical practice on Ratios, he had no idea what a ratio was. He was encouraged to search on the Internet for explanations. He was allowed to refer to the answers at the back of the book after every sum to check that he was on the right track. If the answer was wrong, he was allowed to redo the sum. In the exam preparation stage however, he had to complete a whole math past year exam paper within the allotted time. He could not refer, and he could not redo the sums he had gotten wrong without first totalling the marks. Then, Little Boy and I discussed his mistakes and his exam-smart techniques.

⚲ *Does your process produce concrete deliverables?* At the end of a process, the child should be able to produce a specific piece of work that you can review. This enables you to check progress and learning. When introducing a complicated process that is new, you can ask for easy mini-deliverables so that the child can feel small achievements along the way. For example, when I first introduced the process of memorising Chinese compositions, I required Little Boy to recite to me after every 3 sentences. This was soon lengthened to 4 and then to 5. Before long, he was on his own and all I needed to do was to listen to him read the composition at the end of the day.

Do you ask your child how he feels about his old/new process? This not only helps you to evaluate the process but it trains your child to do so as well. As he got older, Little Boy would give very intelligent suggestions on how he thought he could learn better. I asked Little Boy to score upon 10, the amount of learning he obtained through memorising high quality Chinese compositions, compared to attending Chinese composition writing camp. Little Boy was able to share with me that memorising high quality Chinese compositions was 8/10 of learning intensity compared to his one week Chinese composition writing camp at 2/10 of learning intensity. He explained that memorising Chinese compositions was very intense compared to the fun and games of the Chinese composition writing camp. He explained that he learnt more in less time by memorising Chinese compositions.

Is your process designed for independent monitoring by your child? Being in control is a motivating experience. If a process depends heavily on you to implement then your child will never be able to eventually take full control. For example, I chose to have Grandma read the Chinese compositions into an audio file so that Little Boy could eventually manage his process independently. There was no need to involve Grandma each time. Here is another example. I gave Little Boy full access to all the answer sheets so that he would be in full control of his practices from doing through to marking and evaluation of mistakes.

Is the process too complex for independent monitoring by your child? Being in control is a motivating experience only if your child feels competent enough to manage the process himself. Even small children can manage simple processes with few steps if properly trained. When introducing a new and complex process to Little Boy, I always put aside large chunks of time where I am available to give process feedback. For example, I introduced the process of memorising Chinese compositions during the December holidays. I took time off to see him through the whole process. Once the process was stable, I let him monitor it himself.

Is your process efficient? One of the things I taught Little Boy about designing process was that a process needed to be a "lazy" one (i.e., one where one could learn the fastest by spending the least time... without compromising true learning). Laziness is vastly underrated. When there is so much to learn, then the process that requires the least time (without going as far as cheating) is best. Your child's time is finite and children also need to play. If every minute of your child's time is worth $100, how would you use that time?

Is your process so lazy (or efficient) that it has

become ineffective? It is one thing to take intelligent short cuts. It is another to shortcut the process so drastically that one bypasses critical skills practice.

Informational Feedback

Inspired by the work of Professor Edwin A. Locke and Professor Gary P. Latham.

WHAT IS INFORMATIONAL FEEDBACK?

People often take feedback to mean words like "Good job" or "This was badly done". Informational feedback is none of that. Informational feedback is the provision of accurate and objective information about the activity being undertaken.

If you play computer games, there is a scoreboard that gives you information about the points you have scored, and about the number of lives you have left. If you are playing a sniper game, you get real time information about how well you have been shooting, every time your target on the screen falls backward and dies a bloody death. This is informational feedback and is different from vague

103

compliments or thumps on the back. Informational feedback really tells you how well you are doing. Informational feedback about a math practice is simply the number of sums that have earned a tick, instead of a cross.

Why Give Informational Feedback?

Research shows that informational feedback is in itself motivating[7]. That's why people like to play computer games. Computer games provide real time information to show you how you are doing. People are motivated to better the score. This is also the reason why industrial-organisational psychologists encourage companies to put up large scoreboards inside the factory on team defect rate etc… Just the mere fact of being able to check in on factual progress information is encouraging.

Conversely, it is very discouraging to not have any feedback at all about one's objective progress over a long period of time. Imagine if over a period of 6 months, there is no way for you to get objective information (i.e., sales numbers, customer complaints etc…) on whether you are doing your job right. It would be like working very hard blindly. Most people would be discouraged by that.

Adults typically have a longer time tolerance when it

comes to feedback. In other words, they don't expect to be given informational feedback every five minutes when they are trying to complete a project. Children have a much shorter time outlook. When the task is difficult, children can be discouraged in minutes. When the task is difficult, a shortened feedback loop provides the little infusions of emotional energy that helps a child to persist at the difficult task. One of the things a parent can do when the child faces daunting difficulties, is to shorten the feedback loop. This means that instead of checking their answers after every 10 sums, you may choose to check them every 1 sum instead.

Earlier, I recounted Little Boy's ordeal with 4-digit long division sums. Since Little Boy thought it was an impossible task, I shortened the informational feedback loop to one sum at a time. Where I normally mark his work at the end of the day, I chose on that day, to mark his work after every sum. Getting informational feedback after every sum, stimulated a short burst of emotional energy in his heart. This short burst of emotional energy helped him to persist through the next impossible sum. One by one, until all the sums were done. The next day, when the worst was over, I lengthened the feedback loop to 5 sums at a time, i.e., I only marked his work when he had completed 5 sums.

Eventually, I went back to marking all his work at the end of the day.

Receiving information about how one is progressing at a task helps to draw available energy towards the task. When playing a sniper computer game, every time you shoot down an opponent, you strive to shoot the next. The constant feedback re-focuses your energies and keeps you from getting distracted by everything else around you. Informational feedback holds your attention and focuses it.

CHALLENGES OF GIVING INFORMATIONAL FEEDBACK

Challenge 6.1:   *The Right Task Difficulty*

Informational feedback is only motivating when you can see some progress. The child must experience some hits before he sees a few misses. And then he must experience hits again, before he experiences misses. If the task is way beyond the child's capabilities and the child misses all the time, his enthusiasm will run out, and then he will lose interest and become not motivated at all. If you want to use informational feedback to motivate your child, you need to first evaluate whether the difficulty level of the exercise is just difficult enough to provide enough hits and enough misses. If you think that there will be too many misses, then you must be around to top up the child's emotional energy through the emotional umbilical cord.

Challenge 6.2: *Informational Feedback for Languages*

Informational feedback is easy to give when you are dealing with subjects such as Science and Mathematics, or test formats such as multiple choice questions. A mere tick next to a completed Math sum is informational feedback. A tick next to a Science multiple choice question is sufficient informational feedback.

It is difficult to deliver informational feedback when some measure of subjectivity exists in either the subject content or the testing format. Creative composition writing is not easy to pin down, and if you can't pin it down, it's hard to give factual information about progress in them. However, those of us who can write well, can deconstruct good writing. We know that if we ensure that the text contains a certain set of features, it will be perceived as well written. The trick is to be able to list down these features, describe them to the child and then systematically give feedback on the presence or absence of each.

I now share with readers the set of grading schemes for

creative composition writing that I used to give Little Boy feedback on how well he is writing. This allows me to demonstrate how informational feedback can be given even for subjects that are commonly seen as "subjective".

Writing is a complex process. It can be overwhelming to the child if you address the whole set of features of good writing ALL AT ONCE. As such, readers will note that the grading schemes evolve and change over time and in response to the strengths and weaknesses demonstrated by Little Boy over the years. They also evolved in response to what we slowly discovered about the requirements of the PSLE exam markers.

Grading Scheme 1:   Early Primary 4

By nature, Little Boy is logical and factual. When given a picture composition to do, he'll simply state what happened in a few short sentences and end off with what is likely to happen. His composition plots were predictable and his language factual, and to the point. So I developed a grading scheme as follows...

	Explanation	Marks
Content Interest	A refreshing plot that no one else is likely to think of.	10
5 Power Words and 5 Similes	Difficult words such as "incandescent". Describing using "as ___ as" e.g., "He looked as old as a cricket".	5
Correct Grammar	No grammatical errors.	5

Grading Scheme 2:   Mid Primary 4

Once he understood what was required, Little Boy had no problems generating an interesting storyline. However, his handwriting seriously interfered with my reading. I changed the grading scheme to the following...

	Explanation	Marks
Content Interest	A refreshing plot that no one else is likely to think of.	5
5 Power Words and 5 Similes	Difficult words such as "incandescent". Descriptions using "as ___ as" e.g., "He looked as old as a cricket".	5
Handwriting	Well-formed words that are legible and have adequate spacing.	5
Grammar and Spelling	No grammar or spelling errors.	5

Grading Scheme 3: Early Primary 5

In Primary 5, we realised that the PSLE markers preferred content realism to content interest. Also, 5 power words and 5 similes weren't enough to score well. I changed the grading scheme yet again. This time, I aimed to develop a new focus on Content Realism and also to encourage him to develop a sense of how many difficult words and interesting similes were enough without being overwhelming. Since he had a habit of writing long and convoluted sentences, I added a focus on sentence structure too. So, the grading scheme began to look like this...

	Explanation	Marks
Content Interest	A refreshing plot that no one else is likely to think of.	10
Content Realism	A believable plot with sufficient explanation of loose ends to be logical.	10
Enough Power Words and Similes	Difficult words such as "incandescent". Descriptions using "as ___ as" e.g., "He looked as old as a cricket".	10
Grammar and Spelling	No grammar or spelling errors.	5
Elegant Sentences	Short and simple sentences without too many conjunctions	5

Grading Scheme 4:   Mid Primary 5

In mid-Primary 5, I realised that he didn't bother to flesh out the characters in his story. So, I added that into the marking scheme. I also taught him how to modulate the energy levels in his story and I wanted to see clear contrasts in energy levels as his story progressed.

	Explanation	Marks
Content Interest	A refreshing plot that no one else is likely to think of.	10
Content Realism	A believable plot with sufficient explanation of loose ends to be logical.	10
Enough Power Words and Similes	Difficult words such as "incandescent". Descriptions using "as ___ as" e.g., "He looked as old as a cricket".	5
Start With a Hint of Mystery	Describe a scene but leave out some intriguing details out that will make the reader want to read more.	5
Energy Plotting	Ensure the storyline has 3 levels of energy: Calm, Suspense and Excitement.	5
Grammar and Spelling	No grammar or spelling errors.	5
Characterisation	Vivid description of characters' appearances and personality.	5

Grading Scheme 5:   Early Primary 6

In early Primary 6, another kiasuparents forum member taught me the Rule of 3. I added that into the marking scheme. I took out Content Interest because we realised that Teachers penalised him if his content was too interesting.

	Explanation	Marks
Content Realism	A believable plot with sufficient explanation of loose ends to be logical.	10
Enough Power Words and Similes	Difficult words such as "incandescent". Descriptions using "as ___ as" e.g., "He looked as old as a cricket".	5
Start With a Hint of Mystery	Describe a scene but leave out some intriguing details out that will make the reader want to read more.	5
Energy Plotting	Ensure the storyline has 3 levels of energy: Calm, Suspense and Excitement.	5
Rule of 3	At the peak of excitement, the main character has to try 3 times before succeeding.	5
Grammar and Spelling	No grammar or spelling errors.	5
Characterisation	Vivid description of characters' appearances and personality.	5

I've only given you the major versions of the grading schemes to show you that even for qualitative (as opposed to numerical) work, you can give informational feedback by adding performance foci one at a time. You can also take away foci as and when the child is good enough that he does not need to pay attention there anymore. Along the way, as I marked Little Boy's compositions and felt out his strengths and weaknesses, I tweaked the English composition grading schemes in an infinite number of ways. One of the most memorable grading schemes is captured in the next anecdote.

MINUS 6 UPON 20?

Little Boy had just scored a huge hit in school. He had just topped the class with his English composition, and Teacher had asked him to type out his essay for the class notice board. However, I noticed that he had been careless with some punctuation, and he had neglected to use capital letters at the start of some sentences.

I had talked to him many times before about punctuation and capital letters and I

115

was a little upset that he was still not focusing on them. Little Boy's story lines gripped the attention of the reader, and his vocabulary was evocative. As such, he usually scored well for his English compositions. This gave him the mistaken idea that punctuation and capital letters weren't important. I was determined to correct that mistaken impression. He needed very loud informational feedback about punctuation and capital letters.

I revised my marking scheme to include minus-2 marks for every punctuation error and every missing capital letter. When I graded his next essay, he scored 14/20. As usual, he had good content and nice vocabulary. Then I set about deducting marks for every punctuation error and missing capital letter. His final mark was minus-6 upon 20.

As he went through the essay, he could see "minus 2" in bright red dotted all over. This provided informational feedback about his misses in punctuation and capital letters.

You can be sure that this focused his attention on both, for the next composition. In his next composition, there were no such errors at all. He scored 16 upon 20. This was informational feedback telling him that he had scored a hit. From then onwards, he strove to keep scoring hits as far as punctuation and capital letters were concerned.

Little Boy's school teacher used a very simple marking scheme. There were 2 dimensions only: Content (20 marks) and Language (20 marks). Whilst this scheme might suffice for marking exams quickly to generate marks, it is relatively uninformative with regards to specific aspects of good writing. Looking merely at the marks she gave for Language and Content, Little Boy didn't know what to do to improve either. I therefore devised a more fine-grained marking scheme that served 2 purposes:

- To focus Little Boy's attention on important aspects of good writing during the process of doing the composition.
- To give specific informational feedback about his performance.

HOW TO GIVE INFORMATIONAL FEEDBACK

1. *The age of the child matters when giving informational feedback.* Very young children with short attention spans need frequent feedback to help re-focus attention – perhaps you can choose to mark every half page completed.

2. *The difficulty of the task matters when giving informational feedback.* The more difficult the task, the more discouraging and energy-sapping it is. As such, when a task is very difficult, feedback should be more frequent. To a Primary 2 child, 20 4-digit long division sums look almost impossible to do. For this reason, I marked each sum the moment it was completed.

3. *The prior training of the child's attention span is also an important consideration when trying to determine how often to give feedback.* With training, a child's attention span can be improved beyond what can normally be expected of a child that age. Children with trained and longer attention spans need less frequent informational feedback to re-focus their energies back on the task.

4. *Informational feedback does not need fanfare.* Even if you give the feedback neutrally, it will still work. A

simple and wordless tick next to a completed sum will work fine. If you wish, you can tinge it with positive feelings (i.e., a smile or a happy tone) and you can accompany it with an encouraging phrase such as "Well done." But it is not necessary. Just do not tinge it with negative feelings such as anger, impatience or frustration.

5. *Informational feedback requires you to know exactly what areas you want to see improved.* You design the informational feedback according to the situation. This was what I did in the above examples of the English composition grading schemes.

6. *Teachers in school often use informational feedback to signal to your children the requirements of the PSLE. Don't interfere with their efforts by calling them up to bug them for the extra one or two marks that they have too harshly cut from your child's test paper.* They are using the marks to draw your child's attention to elements that they know will be important in the PSLE. In fact, there were times when Little Boy's teachers were generous in according a mark here, and a mark there, all whilst taking care to comment that PSLE markers would certainly be less lenient. In such

instances, I myself deducted those marks and explained to Little Boy that his work was truly worth fewer marks because of such and such a reason. The important exams are the PSLE. I do not mind losing a mark here and there as long as each loss of mark gives information important for focusing attention on the right thing.

7

RIVR & RIVP

Inspired by the work of Professor Burrhus Frderick Skinner.

WHAT IS BEHAVIOURAL REINFORCEMENT?

A behavioural reinforcement is any pleasant experience that results from a behaviour. The pleasant experience therefore encourages the behaviour. Behavioural psychologists have many different reinforcement schedules. There are schedules where you reinforce every single time a behaviour appears. There are schedules where you reinforce regularly after a fixed time interval. However, to achieve long lasting behavioural change, the best reinforcement schedule to use is **random, intermittent and variable reinforcement (RIVR)**. In other words, one reinforces in a manner that is completely unpredictable.

WHY IS RIVR IMPORTANT?

Random, intermittent and variable reinforcement is the best way to get a child addicted to his studies. We all know how easy it is to get addicted to gambling. It's because gambling provides random, intermittent and variable reinforcement. You win sometimes. It's random. You win intermittently, not regularly. Each time you win, you get different amounts of money. Sometimes you win small. Other times you win big. But when you do win, you experience an intense joy that approaches elation. This intensely happy emotional experience is burnt into your memory circuits. You remember its intense pleasure, and that memory keeps you wanting more.

However, since it happens completely randomly, you can't tell when pulling the jackpot lever will lead to an avalanche of coins. So you keep on pulling the jackpot lever because you keep hoping that the next pull will give you a win. The result is that a person is motivated to keep on gambling in the hope of recapturing the intense joy of winning a gamble. If you are skilful enough, you can use the same strategy to get your child addicted to studying.

A Side Note:
You Mean You Don't Approve Consistently Of Your Child's Good Behaviour? You Approve Only Randomly?

No. That is not what I mean.

The reinforcement is random. The approval is consistent. Reinforcement and approval are not the same thing. I often comment on good behaviour. At other times, I smile a silent approval and then leave. Randomly, I pick Little Boy up and laugh and make a huge fuss about how special he is because he behaved so well.

Hence, when I was teaching Little Boy to be diligent, I made clear to him that diligence meant sitting at his table to complete 4 problem sums without getting distracted. I left him alone to do his work. Once in a while, I would drop in on him. If I saw that he was off task, I would put him back on task with a gentle comment. If I saw that he was on task, I would sometimes pat his head and smile silently into his eyes. At other times, I would open the room door and quietly close it again. He knew I had come in and he knew that I approved of him staying on task. Occasionally, I would interrupt him, give him a big hug and praise him to the highest heavens for his diligence, and then swing him around in my arms.

He enjoyed these moments of being swung in my arms and basking in my praises. He tried harder to stay on task because he was never sure when I would explode into hugs and laughter. Soon, staying on task for 4 problem sums had become a routine habit.

THE CHALLENGES OF USING RIVR

Challenge 7.1:   *Knowing Your Child*

It is challenging to choose the correct RIVR. Children are built differently. The parent needs to know the child well enough to choose an RIVR that the child perceives as highly positive.

Challenge 7.2:   *Being There to Catch the Moment*

RIVR is most effective when there is a tight link between demonstrated behaviour and the positive reinforcement. This is usually accomplished by reinforcing immediately. To reinforce behaviours immediately, one has to be present when the behaviours are being enacted. For many parents, this is difficult to achieve.

HOW TO DO RIVR?

1. When people associate a behaviour with a very positive experience, they will want to repeat the behaviour. Naturally occurring positive experiences occur at random within the study process. They can be anything from successfully completing a difficult piece of work, to reading a funny comprehension passage, to having your English composition read out by Teacher in class.

One cannot predict the when and where of such positive experiences. *When you see a naturally occurring positive experience, celebrate it with your child and increase the intensity of his positive experience. Turn his happiness into exhilaration by sharing his joy.* It is at high levels of positive emotional intensity that addictions are most likely to take root.

2. *Make it intense.* The reinforcement needs to be a highly intense emotional experience. It needs to stimulate the kind of joy that is close to mentally orgasmic. The intensity of the positive emotional experience is memorable and addictive. It is this remembered joy that keeps people wanting more.

3. *Don't offer bribes to create a positive experience.* When you offer money for performance, effort will dip when you stop offering money or toy rewards. When Little Boy solves a difficult Math problem, I don't pay him. I don't want him to associate his happiness with the toy or money bribe. I want him to associate his happiness with the study process. The toy or money reward has too tangible, too real a presence. Such tangible distractions dilute the association between happiness and achievement. Instead of thinking his joy is due to

having achieved something, the child begins to believe that he is happy because of the toy. Any touchable, feelable reward will prevent the child from savouring the pure joy of achievement and getting addicted to the joy of achievement.

4. *Instead of toys and money, stand ready to intensify naturally occurring positive experiences in the study process.* One person being happy alone is less joyful than two persons celebrating together. The positive experiences naturally occurring in the study process are more intense when you share it with your child. Celebrate his triumphs with many congratulations and plenty of hugs.

5. *Instead of toys and money, create other positive experiences that do not have a physical form.* Once, when Little Boy had worked really well, I gave him three days of pure play time (out of the blue). That really put him in seventh heaven. Another time, I simply took unplanned leave to spend time with him. This again got Little Boy so happy that he was jumping up and down the chairs. Unlike money or a physical toy, these positive experiences are intangible and possess no physical form. *In the child's mind, the*

resulting gladness from a highly positive experience with no tangible form can be easily associated with the study process. They begin feel happy about studying, in the same way that Pavlov's dog was conditioned to salivate at the sound of a bell (because Pavlov rang a bell every time he fed his dog). Indeed, in an earlier chapter on providing structured choices, I recounted how I managed to get a Little Boy who didn't like to read, to love reading. Here is an adapted excerpt from the earlier story that illustrates how I intensified a positive experience in such a way, that Little Boy became addicted to reading English books.

GETTING ADDICTED TO READING

Little Boy hated books. Every time, I tried to read to him, he yawned and then he tried to toddle away.

So, in Primary 2, I devised a process where Little Boy was required to read a certain number of books every week. At first, Little Boy read the books he had chosen because in choosing the books, he owned his choices. Soon, as I knew would invariably happen, some books gave him real pleasure. He laughed through some, and he was captivated by the action and suspense in others. Then one morning, he picked up a Secret Seven book without being told to. He was so captivated that he only answered me in monosyllables that whole morning.

I decided to strike whilst the iron was hot. I proposed then and there to bring him to the bookstore to buy the whole series of Secret Seven books. We came home with the entire series of The Spiderwick Chronicles, Secret Seven and Famous Five. It burned a hole in my pocket but that afternoon, I put a downpayment on my son's love affair with English literature... Coming back in the car, you could tell that he felt like he had won the lottery. That rush of intense joy that came with suddenly (1) owning a mound of new possessions (2) spending a whole lazy afternoon with his beloved Mother, became all confused with books, the tangible and feel-able books in the plastic bag.

On that day, Little Boy's brain formed a strong positive association between books and happiness. Even today, when Little Boy is sad, he will find solace in a book. He is addicted to books, and to think that there was a time when I despaired of him because every time I tried to read to him, he yawned and toddled away.

WHAT IS BEHAVIOURAL PUNISHMENT?

A behavioural punishment is any unpleasant experience that arises because of a behaviour. It therefore discourages the behaviour. Again, to be effective, behavioural punishment needs to be random, intermittent and variable (i.e., RIVP). RIVP can occur naturally in instances where a behaviour results in unpleasant consequences. For example, using a stick to hit tree branches in a park usually is harmless except when there is a beehive on the branch. Getting stung by bees is a naturally occurring RIVP that is so intensely painful that it would discourage a person from hitting tree branches with a stick in future. Note that in RIVP, just like in RIVR, the reinforcement needs to be random, intermittent, variable and highly intense in order to be effective. RIVP can also be used deliberately to discourage behaviours.

Why Is RIVP Important?

When people associate a behaviour with a very negative experience, they will stop that behaviour soon enough. I used to park our family's second car in a slot meant only for our first car. The condominium rule book states that a family's second car needs to be parked in Basement 2 of the underground car park. I would consistently park it in Level 1 because I was naughty. In a space of 1.5 years, I had three flat tires. Each flat tire cost me about $200 to replace. The pain I felt was moderately intense. It didn't happen every time I parked in a slot meant for first cars only. It happened randomly. However, when it did happen, it was very painful for me. It didn't take long for me to learn to park where I should.

Just in case.

RIVP is highly effective in discouraging undesirable behaviours. Hypothetically, if you had a husband who loved to womanise, a course of RIVP using painful (but harmless) electric shocks would be quite effective in reconditioning him. This is provided that there is no way for him to tell which woman he tries to seduce is a mole planted especially to administer those shocks suddenly and without warning. After a few random and very painful experiences, he'll be put off womanising for quite a while.

Of course, no one does that to husbands. RIVP is effective but if used without moral judgment (or self-control), can be unethical. We certainly don't want to be unethical. Not surprisingly, many parents disapprove of traditional RIVP techniques such as caning and pinching. There are serious ethical considerations when one decides to cause pain to a child. RIVP arises from a long tradition of research and practice in behavioural modification theory[8] (some of the research done in the past was indeed unethical and did actually employ electric shocks on animals).

However, whatever your moral stand on this issue, RIVP is only effective when intensely painful. In view of this, I was in two minds about including the present section on RIVP. However, I considered that whether or not this section is included in this book, there will be parents who believe in punishment. If one must punish, one should learn to do it properly (and rarely), so as to avoid inflicting unnecessary pain. I finally decided to include RIVP in this book so that parents who already do use traditional RIVP techniques can learn to use them wisely, and not cause more pain than necessary when discouraging undesirable behaviours.

A working knowledge of RIVP is also useful for another reason. It is useful for parents to know about RIVP because it occurs naturally in school. The child could have failed to understand a topic being taught. He could have been unfairly scolded by a well-meaning Teacher. He could have been terrorised by a class bully. All these are random, intermittent and variable negative experiences that the child invariably will go through in school. When these negative experiences crop up, the parent needs to step in quickly to neutralise the negative experience before they create in the child, an aversion to school.

Lastly, I have yet to meet a parent who has never scolded/punished a child. However, I have met parents who scold/punish without method. When something is done without method, there can be unintended consequences. It is good to learn how and when to enact RIVP properly in order to avoid…

♀ … scolding and punishing the child ineffectively. Ineffective scoldings and punishments inflict pain on the child with no results to show for the pain.

135

Ⓥ   ... scolding and punishing the child too often. Ineffective scoldings and punishments usually lead to more scoldings and punishments. Overly frequent scoldings and punishments will damage the emotional connection between parent and child. This will in turn make it difficult for a parent to feed emotional encouragement to the child in times of need. Furthermore, when the emotional connection is strong, it becomes easier to exert strong but gentle control over the child.

Ⓥ   ... having to live a lonely life as an abandoned parent of grown-up children who can remember nothing but scoldings and punishment throughout their childhood.

THE CHALLENGES OF NEUTRALISING OR USING RIVP

Challenge 7.1:   *Keeping in Touch*

Many parents have no time to keep in touch with the daily events that happen in school. Unless one makes an effort to ask about the child's day, many instances of RIVP can go unnoticed, and as time wears on, the child learns to dislike school and it becomes difficult to reverse the negative effects of RIVP.

Challenge 7.2:   *What is the Right RIVP?*

Next, the choice of RIVP can be challenging. It requires the parent to figure out what the child dislikes. Some kids don't mind physical pain but they hate being ignored. The parent needs to know the child well enough to be able to choose the correct RIVP.

Challenge 7.3:   *Overusing RIVP*

Lastly, there is a tendency for some parents to use RIVP at the slightest excuse. This is to be avoided because it can damage the emotional connection between parent and child; and a strong emotional connection is essential in order to help the parent feed emotional energy to the child when the child encounters disappointments and discouragement. The emotional connection between parent and child is crucial in any motivation endeavour. Even RIVP, when done by a parent with no emotional connection with a child, will not work. This is because the child is too busy hating the parent, and not focusing on resolving undesired behaviours.

RIVP is to be used sparingly.

A Side Note:
You Mean You Don't Correct Your Child's Bad Behaviour
Consistently? You Do It Only Randomly?

No. That is not what I mean.

The punishment is random. The correction is not. Punishment and correction are not the same thing. I have a long fuse with my children. Days and months can go by where I comment neutrally that Little Boy should jog after school. This is correction. Little Boy is a little couch potato. However, blood flow to the brain enhances cognitive performance. Hence, I corrected Little Boy's reluctance to jog every day for 12 months. They were gentle and patient corrections.

Then one day, out of the blue, I exploded. The performance shattered the peace in our neighbourhood. 3 heads popped up at the backyard fence to watch the fireworks. 2 pairs of eyes peeked through the front garden hedge wonderingly. The punishment was memorable but completely random. There was no way for Little Boy to see this coming. I was gentle all the way up to the day before the massive explosion. It seemed random to him.

Parents usually give ample warning of an impending explosion. They begin to look exasperated with every new reminder to behave (i.e., corrective action). Their tone of voice changes over time as they keep reminding their child (i.e., corrective action). The child is smart enough to keep up the misbehaviour until just before you explode. I am completely calm right up until the explosion.

As such, the explosion looks quite random. There is no way to predict its occurrence. The explosion is also memorably painful. If something memorably painful happens to you for misbehaving and you cannot predict its occurrence (apart from knowing that it is due to your misbehaviour), you will make sure you stop misbehaving quickly.

How To Do RIVP

1. *Never administer RIVP when you are angry.* Always do it when you are in full control of yourself, to avoid inflicting more pain than necessary.

2. *It is important to tailor the RIVP to the undesired behaviour.* Undesired behaviours that are less ingrained, can be discouraged by less severe RIVP. RIVP can be as gentle as a frown if the behaviour is not ingrained.

3. *The thing to remember in effective RIVP is random, intermittent and variable.* If you punish regularly and predictably, the behaviour comes back the moment you stop the punishment schedule. If you punish the undesired behaviour only sometimes, there is no way the child can tell which incident of a specific undesired behaviour you will decide to punish. He will thus keep on trying to avoid punishment just in case. 99% of the time, my children's misbehaviours are addressed with gentle reminders and attempts at reasoning. I would have tried every other method to mould behaviour before I resort to a Mother Medusa tantrum (i.e., RIVP). On average, I throw a Mother Medusa tantrum about once every 2 or 3 years, and always for behaviours that

I have been working on for months or even years. But every time I throw a tantrum, it comes as a complete surprise, and seems completely random simply because my child has come to expect another sweet and gentle reminder that so characterises our interactions.

4. *It is important to use RIVP only very sparingly.* Overused, it can damage the emotional connection you have with your child. This prevents you from feeding your child with the emotional encouragement he might need in other instances through the emotional connection. Between emotional connection and RIVP, I have obtained far more mileage using emotional connection than RIVP. Hence, I would never choose to sacrifice emotional connection by overusing RIVP.

10 FEET TALL WITH HORNS!!

Little Boy wasn't born diligent. He learnt to be diligent thanks to a combination of RIVR (praises and hugs) and RIVP (banshee like yellings that last 2.5 hours).

Diligence is an essential part of studying. Diligence is an important skill and contributes to academic success, especially with children who are neither gifted nor very smart.

That's us, and our children.

Like any other little boy, my Little Boy believed work to be a necessary evil. You do it when you have to. You do it when you remember to. It is more convenient to forget to do work. If one can get away with it, why not? Instead of hanging around to make sure he did his homework each time, I was rather haphazard in my supervision. Sometimes, I would sit there to make sure he does his work. Sometimes, I would disappear and then come back to check. Sometimes, I would disappear and not even check. It seemed completely random.

Invariably, there would be moments where I caught him actually doing his work. Then I would hop around with exuberant joy and praise him "I have such a special son. Mine is the best son in the world. I don't know of anyone else's son who would at such a young age sit there and complete work without being nagged at."

141

Little Boy was still a wee little one then. Hence there were also moments where I caught him goofing off. Sometimes, when I saw that, I would gently tell him off and ask him to go back to work. Once however, I grew by 10 feet, developed horns, pushed forth fangs dripping with blood and give him a loud and long scolding, lasting 2 hours. I went on and on about me wasting my life, and being heartbroken... and how could a big boy like him behave thus!?

Drama Queen doesn't even begin to describe what I did in my performance. I amazed myself with how long I could go on about the same thing using different words in different sentences, pausing 5 seconds in between to rest.

However, such a performance needs to be very rare or it loses its power to change behaviour. Children, like anyone else, can become immune to hysterics. Besides, it is hard to maintain a strong emotional connection with a constantly hysterical mom.

The contrast between the Mother Theresa and Mother Medusa was so great that Little Boy had every motivation to quit the laziness and embrace the diligence, if only to keep the Mother Medusa from coming back. The effects were all the more impactful in that I went from 100% good to 100% evil in 30 seconds flat. There was no lead up to the explosion. One minute, I was calm. I came. I looked. The next, I was standing there with sharp teeth, horns and 10 feet tall with mouth wide open and unmentionable sounds pouring forth in an endless stream of vituperative words.

Whoa!

Between the random praises and hugs and the completely random mega explosion, Little Boy learnt that it was much nicer to be caught doing his work than goofing off, just in case Mother Medusa came back.

5. *When you use RIVP, link the punishment very clearly to a very specific undesirable behaviour.* That way,

your child develops an aversion to only that specified behaviour. If you fail to be specific enough, then the child may associate the entire study process with the RIVP. As a result, he may dislike studying as a whole. Worse still, the child may associate the RIVP with you and develop an aversion to you.

6. *Another way of using RIVP is to allow the life situation to punish your child once in a while.* Life situations are in themselves random, intermittent and variable, since no 2 situations are exactly alike. This is RIVP *au naturel*. In the next anecdote, I will illustrate how one can use RIVP *au naturel* to good effect.

THE EVIL MOTHER'S EVIL PLAN

Little Boy was supposed to do 4 problem sums every afternoon, after school. It was a rather simple schedule to follow, I thought. Even a little doggie can manage a simple schedule like "Eat 1 bowl of food every afternoon" eh?

But well, Little Boy didn't do his 4 problem sums every afternoon. Yes... yes... Little Boy was still a small wee one. His voice was still squeaky and he was still afraid of the dark. At that age, nobody understands the value of diligence. Every little boy at that age wants to play. Little Boy believed that work was a necessary evil invented by me. So, I hatched a plot to show him that I didn't invent homework, and that he needed to be diligent.

I watched him skive silently. As I sat there typing my consultancy and research reports, I silently watched as he frittered many afternoons away digging for snails in the garden, catching beetles to feed his pitcher plant, making believe that an ice-cream stick was a fighter plane out on a mission to bomb the ants. My, my, what fun!

In my Evil Mother's heart, I said "Heh! Heh! Heh! You will regret these moments of joyful play, my Little Boy. Heh! Heh! Heh! The day will come when you will regret your lack of diligence."

4 days before his Math exam, the Evil Mother unleashed her Evil Plan on her playful and un-diligent son. The Evil Mother (that's

me!) printed out the most difficult practice exam paper she could find and proposed cheerfully, "Hey Little Boy, exams are in 4 days, maybe you should do this exam practice?" Predictably, Little Boy did very poorly. He was stressed and very demoralised. Little Boy sweated from his brow and quaked in his shoes. Yup... he certainly was regretting those days in the sun catching beetles and bombing ants. The Evil Mother's Evil Plan was to allow Little Boy to go into his exam and do badly, in order to be able to say "Hmmmm... it's your own fault for not doing your 4 problem sums every afternoon diligently" (Psssst... note how the Evil Mother ties the misbehaviour tightly to the RIVP).

However, the Kind Mother (that's me!) fought with the Evil Mother (that's also me!) and won. The Kind Mother decided that it would be too cruel to actually allow Little Boy to fail an exam. She took over and worked with Little Boy to help him catch up on all the time wasted bombing ants with ice-cream sticks.

In 4 days, they did math drill after math drill. Little Boy spent hours trying to achieve speed and accuracy. It was very tiring and all through those 4 days, Little Boy was scared silly. Even on the eve of the math exam, he was scared silly. Every once in a while, the Evil Mother popped out again and said "If you had diligently done your 4 problem sums every afternoon, you wouldn't have to suffer now." (Psssst… note again how the Evil Mother ties the misbehaviour tightly to the RIVP). But mostly, the Kind Mother provided a lot of courage through the Emotional Connection.

On the day he received his results, he was disappointed. He had only scored 80-something marks when he had wanted to score 90-something. This gave the Evil Mother something to talk about when Little Boy got home. Little Boy was sad. Happily, the Kind Mother came along, hugged Little Boy and said, "The next time, I am sure you will do better, because the next time, I am sure you will be diligent."

And Little Boy nodded his head.

Following that, Little Boy made a credible effort to keep to his work schedule. He was still a small wee one and sometimes needed reminding. The Kind Mother reminded him once in a while elbowing the Evil Mother out of the way, saying "Can't you see he is making an effort? We can surely help him a little bit?!"

By the time the next Math exam came around, Little Boy had done so many practices that he wasn't stressed at all. The Kind Mother proposed "You seem pretty prepared eh? Why don't you take time off to play for 3 days before the Math exam? This will help you relax." Little Boy was overjoyed. He declared "Mom, I like it when exams come around. It's so relaxing." This time, he topped the class in Math.

7. If you choose to allow the life situation to punish your child once in a while, *never ever spite the child.* Watch your body language and tone carefully. Your child has

just been hurt by RIVP *au naturel*. Your miserable child is going to come to you for comfort. Don't spite the child. Don't gloat like a goat and say "Obigood chachagood!" (Singaporean playground lingo for "Good for you that you got hurt"). Just take the child on your lap and explain the link between his misbehaviour and the logical and unpleasant consequence. Explain how the unpleasant consequence can be avoided in future. Then comfort the child sincerely and lovingly. The naturally occurring RIVP hurts enough. The parent can take the opportunity to be Mr Nice Guy whilst having used the situation to administer a targeted punishment. It's good to be Mr Nice Guy as much as possible because this preserves the Emotional Connection between you and your child... and the Emotional Connection is THE most important motivational strategy in this whole book.

8. *RIVPs also occur naturally during the study process without any help from you, and they can discourage your child's love for school. This means that one needs to closely monitor the child's experience at school in order to identify instances of RIVP that could cause a*

child to dislike school. In the next family anecdote, I will illustrate how a bully was responsible for making Little Boy dislike school, and how I stepped in to neutralise the negative experience.

THE GORILLA

Little Boy was a puny thing in Primary 2. He was in the same class as another boy who looked something like a gorilla with no fur. The Gorilla went around threatening every other child in the class. Parent after parent complained, and so The Gorilla's seat was moved all around the tables like a gypsy camp.

One day, The Gorilla ended up sitting next to Little Boy. When Little Boy came home pale and quiet one day, I knew something was wrong. He explained to me that The Gorilla had threatened to kick him in the crotch, and had pushed him up against the wall. Poor Little Boy was terrified.

For two months, Little Boy tolerated The Gorilla. Every day, when he came home, I would ask him about The Gorilla. Together,

we devised creative strategies worthy of Sun
Tzu's Art of War. You see, I wanted Little Boy
to learn to cope with bullies in life. However,
the lesson came at a price. Little Boy's grades
suffered, and he began to dread going to
school. His Teacher began to complain about
sloppy work and inattentiveness. These were
all signs of a distracted and unhappy child - a
child who disliked school.

I encouraged Little Boy along every day
and offered emotional encouragement every
day after school, through our Emotional
Connection. I explained that the worst thing
that could happen would be to get a real
punch in the face. And if that happened, he
was not allowed to punch back. He was to
come home to me with evidence of black eye
and bleeding nose, and I would do the rest.

And then I waited. I waited like a
Machiavelli for The Gorilla to make a very bad
mistake that would get him tied him up by
the ankles to the school hall rafters and have
him publicly caned by hooded men wearing

leather aprons. Mwahahahaha!

I had thought that The Gorilla would give Little Boy a black eye or something. He didn't. He committed daylight robbery instead. The Gorilla divested Little Boy of a textbook. He rubbed off Little Boy's name (written in pencil) and wrote his own on the book (with a pen). However, I knew that the pencil markings had left grooves on the page. I marched to school and complained about theft, and made very clear that it was a crime, and that The Gorilla was a criminal.

After examining the evidence, one Teacher threw her voice clear across the canteen and proposed to administer a public caning in the school hall. The Gorilla reinstated the stolen book to Little Boy and promised not to terrorise him again. And then I asked that The Gorilla's seat be moved away.

Little Boy told me after school that day that he would never fear The Gorilla again because The Gorilla was even more fearful of the Teachers than he (Little Boy) had ever been. It was a nice little triumph for Little Boy. However, if not for my intervention, Little Boy would have learnt to hate school. Firstly, he would have hated school because of The Gorilla's incessant bullying. Secondly, because he was so distracted, he couldn't keep up with his work. Then, Little Boy would have learnt to hate school because he could not keep up.

I later heard that The Gorilla was sent for professional counselling, and that he was much improved without ever having been tied to the rafters by his ankles, and caned by men wearing black hoods. Drat! This said, we later learnt that The Gorilla had come from a highly dysfunctional home. Poor thing!

8 | Strengthen Self-Efficacy: Difficult Victories™

Inspired by the work of Professor Albert Bandura.

WHAT IS SELF-EFFICACY?

Psychologists define this to be beliefs about one's capability to produce given levels of performance. A child with strong self-efficacy beliefs about school will persist longer in the face of difficulties. One mustn't confuse this with self-esteem, which is a sense of self-worth.

They are 2 very different psychological realities.

Self-efficacy beliefs have a very specific target and differ with different target activities. Self-esteem does not differ with target activities. If you have high self-esteem, you have high self-esteem all the time. It doesn't matter if you are baking cakes or planting a garden. Feelings of self-efficacy have a target. For example, I have low self-efficacy beliefs about making puff pastry, but I have high self-efficacy beliefs about motivating a child who is completely uninterested in studying. I know I will certainly fail at making puff pastry but I am confident enough that I can make any child (barring those with learning disabilities) want to study. Any child at all.

WHY STRENGTHEN SELF-EFFICACY?

Motivation researcher, Professor Gary P. Latham wrote, "Given the same low level of performance, people with high self-efficacy exert effort and persist until they have mastered the task, whereas those with low self-efficacy view their poor performance as a reason to abandon their goal" [9].

School is difficult. If school were easy, there would be no need to go there. All things being equal, the child who exerts effort and persists will get better results than another (perhaps more intelligent) who has given up when he encounters difficulty, for difficulty there surely will be. Research documents that high self-efficacy is developed in 3 ways[10] (1) when other people believe you can, (2) when you observe a role model who could, and (3) when you have experienced your own Difficult Victories™. Of the 3 ways, the most effective way to develop high self-efficacy is to experience your own Difficult Victories™. So that is what we will start looking at in this chapter.

WHAT ARE DIFFICULT VICTORIES™?

Difficult Victories™ are achievements that almost didn't happen, or happened after great and long effort by the child (not you!). These experiences of difficult victory do not need to start in primary school or be limited to schoolwork. A strong belief in one's ability to overcome difficult challenges can be developed from babyhood through activities such as buckling the shoes, buttoning the shirt, putting a spoonful of yoghurt into the mouth without spilling a drop, or sucking an orange till dry.

THE MISFIRING THUMB

The Daughter was all of 2 months old. She had developed red skin all around her mouth. It didn't seem to itch, nor was there any peeling. I couldn't figure out what was wrong.

Then I noticed that she had picked up the habit of staring intently at her thumb. There she was, holding out her thumb like a

159

drunken cowboy would raise a shaky pistol. This alone took so much effort that her eyes crossed. Then, she began the slow and unsteady process of trying to fit her thumb into her mouth. This was easier said than done. More often than not, she only managed to jab her thumb onto the sides of her mouth. On more than one occasion, she forgot to open her mouth. There were so many body parts to co-ordinate just to get one thumb into one mouth. As I stood there watching her, I realised the extreme difficulty of the endeavour. It was as difficult for her as it would be for me to hit a volleyball without the ball hitting me.

She was extraordinarily persistent, The Daughter was. I suppose that thumb really tasted good. She tried for a full 15 minutes before she managed to get her thumb into her mouth. If you ask any child waiting for his ice-cream, 15 minutes is an eternity. I was impatient just looking at her. It was all I could do to stop myself from grabbing her hand and

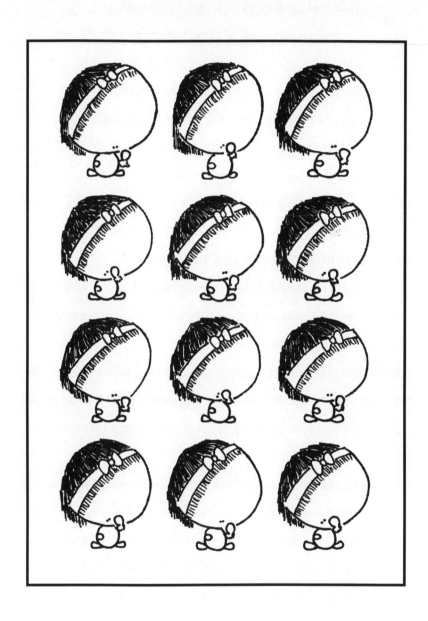

putting that tiny thumb into her mouth.

However, I waited. I was there to witness the momentous occasion of her thumb successfully reaching her mouth. I made a big fuss over her and praised her profusely. Unfortunately, my joy was short-lived because we found it extremely difficult to break the thumb-sucking habit later.

WHY EXPERIENCE DIFFICULT VICTORIES™?

Difficult Victories™ develop self-efficacy. A child with very high self-efficacy faces down difficulties without giving up. This child is motivated to keep on trying no matter the difficulty. The entire school experience is fraught with challenges. High self-efficacy prevents the child from giving up or running away from the challenges he meets in school.

Even though self-efficacy is target-specific (as I mentioned above), the accumulated experience of Difficult Victories™ over the years, builds the general belief that difficulties of any sort can be conquered. It builds general self-efficacy. This is especially so when a child has had a few experiences of achieving what he initially believed to be impossible. Achieving impossible goals builds very high self-efficacy.

Readers may be laughing out loud at this point at the ridiculous notion of doing impossible things. If it is impossible, it cannot be done, right? I too laughed out loud when this notion was put to me. This notion is not documented anywhere in research as yet, but I can assure you that in Singapore there is at least one organisation that believes in setting impossible goals for employees as a matter of routine. And employees achieve these goals as a matter of routine without en masse resignations. Indeed, some employees have worked there for 15 years, and they think the impossible is normal. I know because for 2 years I conducted research on employee motivation in that organisation.

New employees in that organisation came into interviews wide-eyed and incredulous, explaining in graphic terms that they had been given goals that they didn't think they could achieve. However, employees who had worked there for more than 3 years hemmed and hawed when I asked them about impossible goals and then they would say... "I wouldn't say 'impossible'. I have been here so long and I've done really difficult stuff that I had thought impossible so…. Ummmm… It's just…. Ummmm… difficult. I don't know if I can, but it's worth a try. Just in case I can." One long-time employee actually shrugged his shoulders and said "Impossible? Been there. Done that. Many times."

To give you an idea of how difficult some goals were, here is an example, which I have previously mentioned. A relatively new engineering graduate was given the task of developing a test that would detect a random error in the manufacturing line. The random error was likely to happen once in 20 years. However, if it did happen, it would be a major disaster and the company could lose millions every time it happened. The poor lady had never even been an engineer on the manufacturing line. She worked in the HR Department as a training executive. At that time, existing tests for that specific random error cost a 5-figure sum. She was to devise a test that would cost no more than $200.

It sounded like major R&D work to me! And it was. The poor almost-fresh graduate (with no research degree and no experience on the manufacturing line) ran around the universities looking for help. She chose to go to work at night when the manufacturing line was less busy. She pored through research papers and in her words "At the deepest and darkest point, I would wake up at 1 am... and at 2 am, I am awake. When I next look at the clock it is 3 am. All the time, I think to myself 'Tomorrow, I will go in and tell my boss that I want out. I resign. I can't do it."

But she didn't resign.

She achieved her seemingly impossible goal. I researched into employee motivation inside that organisation for 2 years. It was such a strange organisation in that almost everyone had a similar story to tell. I interviewed people in other organisations and was lucky to get even one such story after hours and hours of probing.

It was such a special place. I learnt so much there. I learnt how the organisation managed to get their employees to commit to delivering the impossible goals. I learnt how the organisation supported and maintained such a culture. I learnt how people managed themselves when the going gets so tough, you see no end in sight. I took these lessons and I converted them into strategies to motivate my children.

On hindsight, I begin to see things clearly. Practically every thing worth doing in the world around us looked impossible at the start. If you were born in the 1700s, would you believe men could one day fly? Cure for cancer?

Cure for AIDS? Internet? There was a time when doctors maintained that it was impossible for the human body to run a mile in under 4 minutes[11]. Present day athletes do it all the time.

Anything worth doing looked impossible at one point. Yet, someone did it because someone believed he could do the impossible. He believed it long enough to try just as long as it took to get it done. On hindsight, I asked myself, "Just what is so laughable about believing one can do the impossible?" Humankind has a track record of impossible doings, beginning with the Little Engine that Could[12], which we read to all our children.

If you can develop in your child self-efficacy so strong that he faces down every difficulty by calling it merely "difficult" and not really "impossible", then you have a child that is motivated to keep on trying no matter the difficulty. In school, there are bound to be difficulties. It is important to keep trying long enough to taste success and allow success to motivate you.

Can You Top the Class in Chinese?
By this point in this book, the reader must have realised that Little Boy's Achilles Heel is

Chinese. Chinese is the only subject where he actually fears to fail. Chinese is the subject that he spends the greatest amount of time on, and yet it is the subject where he consistently scores either below average in class or average at best. Chinese is our nemesis.

I put it to Little Boy in early Primary 6. What do you think of trying to top the class in Chinese? Mind you, we were still a long, long way from the top of the class. He had scored only 79 marks at the end of Primary 5 when the highest mark for Chinese in his class was comfortably above 90. But Little Boy didn't bat an eyelid.

He said, "That's the good thing about what you made me do Mom... you know... when you got me to write out from memory that 2000 word Chinese Model Composition? It was really difficult but I did it in the end. I guess if I have enough time I'll be able to top the class in Chinese. Not now, but maybe at the end of this year?"

The thing about choosing a task like memorising a Chinese Model Composition is that given enough time and persistence, it is NOT impossible. It's impossible only if you give up. Yet, such a task sure does a good job at disguising itself as impossible. These are the types of impossible (but not really impossible tasks) that are a sure-win in your journey to build persistence in your child through having him experience Difficult Victories™.

If you can use Emotional Connection, Informational Feedback and all the other techniques in the preceding chapters to encourage your child and keep him on task, victory over such types of tasks is certain. And once the child has experienced the victory, he or she will internalise the unreasoning but very strong feeling that given enough time, nothing is impossible. Remember, it is feeling that motivates. Not reason. Such a child won't get discouraged easily. He won't give up easily. He'll keep trying till he gets it. I ought to mention that this is also an important life attitude.

CHALLENGES OF PROVIDING DIFFICULT VICTORIES™

Challenge 8.1:   *Let Me Help*

Many parents are impatient. The baby is taking too long to

buckle her shoe. She can't do it. Let me do it for her. Perhaps that is why Someone invented the Terrible Twos, Threes and Fours where children want to do everything their way. The child's psyche knows what it needs to develop – self-efficacy, and pushes the child to insist on doing things for himself and his way. But when a parent butts in to help a child, the child is forced to give up something worth doing. Over-helpful and over-protective parents teach children that some things are impossible for them. If you have time to wait for your child to take forever to do something simple, don't assume too quickly that the child needs help. These little easy things are great occasions to teach children that if they try hard enough, they'll get there. In addition, little children enjoy that little bit of triumph over their little worlds. Let them savour their little triumphs. These experiences get them addicted early to the energy rush that comes with achievement.

The Difficult Victories™ of toddlerhood can seem so paltry that we often forget that they are Difficult Victories™ to the child. Some awareness of how challenging simple tasks look to a child, can go some way in helping adults patiently wait for the child to succeed; and celebrate these events when they happen.

Tasks that little toddlers fail at are so simple that given time, parental encouragement and natural physical development, the child eventually succeeds. For sure! Tying shoelaces. Putting on a pair of shorts. Climbing on a chair to wash one's own hands. They almost always begin by not being able. There almost always are misses. Then, if they persist at it, they will succeed. Hence, don't take these little triumphs away from the little ones. Stand there, watch and cheer them as they conquer these mini-mountains themselves. Parents just need to learn to wait.

Where school is concerned, this applies to packing bags, keeping track of homework and filing. It may be faster to help the child but it's better to be patient and give the child space to fail a few times at these tasks because eventually, success will be sweet. Further, these are fundamental study skills that will empower your child to take charge of his scholastic career.

Challenge 8.2:   *Parents Fear Too Much*
Other parents fear so much for their children that they expend great effort in protecting their children from failure. One can lower one's expectations, setting them only at levels where one knows the child can comfortably achieve.

However, in so doing, parents deny their children the exhilarating experience of almost failing, but actually succeeding. This is an experience full of intense joy, and such intense joy is so addictive that once associated with an activity, the child feels compelled towards that activity just to feel that rush of sweet joy. This rush of sweet joy cannot be experienced unless there was a risk of failure in the first instance, or when a child did actually fail at first but persisted long enough to overcome the failure and achieve his goal.

To give the experience of Difficult Victories™, parents must allow the child to risk failure and also experience actual failure, and be there to encourage the child to try again. If the achievement is too easy, success doesn't build self-efficacy. This is especially difficult to do in primary school. Parents can understand the syllabus and go to great lengths to help their children. In this manner, the child has never really had to experience or face possible failure on his own. As such, he doesn't know how to appreciate his achievements in lower primary even though he may top the class. Success is sweeter when one has tasted some failure before. In the following family anecdote, I will share how addictive success is after one has tasted failure.

171

CONQUERING EARLY FAILURES EMPOWER THE CHILD

I went and dug out The Daughter's report book. The Daughter scored 79 for English, 88 for Math in Primary 1. She placed in the bottom 25% of her YEAR. However, in P1 she scored 99% for Chinese because Grandma plied her with assessment books. Little Boy's grades followed the same pattern i.e., in Primary 1, they were lacklustre to say the least.

English, Math and Science were my subjects to coach. Chinese was Grandma's. We took very different approaches. I looked past the grades in Primary 1 & Primary 2 for both my kids. In Primary 1 & Primary 2 my objectives were (1) they get used to school, (2) they adapt well socially, (3) they learn basic self-management skills, (4) they kinda keep up, (5) they like learning (6) they understand the value of diligence and discipline, (7) they take full ownership of their studies and (8) they experience failure without losing hope.

These were all specific qualitative aims I

had in mind. Not quantifiable, but I wanted to focus on laying this foundation so that I would have a strong foundation of work ethic and self-management skills to build on in Upper Primary.

Primary 1 & 2: Foundational Study Skills & Attitudes

I expected my kids to pack their bags, take notes, keep track of homework etc... That's tough, you know, for the little ones. So many times, they forgot their books. Little Boy lost his exam schedule and I didn't help him get another. For 3 weeks, he went to school wondering miserably whether he would be tested that day, and what that test might be.

So many times, my children failed at these basic tasks that their grades suffered.

I gave very few practice exercises to them at this stage. If they remembered to do their homework, I was happy. My kids "failed" at this stage but neither really failed as in score below 50/100. I did not allow that to happen.

I made sure I did enough academic coaching to maintain their grades at levels that would not prejudice their future efforts to catch up.

Primary 3 & 4: Transiting From Skills and Attitude Focus to Grades Focus

By Primary 3, they pretty much got the hang of the skills required to keep one's head afloat in school. At the very least, they could pack their bags and they owned their study process. So, at about Primary 3, I began to set challenging grade goals (90+ for every subject).

At first, neither kid believed they were capable. Till then, they had only watched wistfully as other students in their class aced exams and topped the class. I am sure they secretly wished that they too were capable. Little Boy memorably commented "I am not one of those who can do well in Math, Mommy."

I began to propose drills, using structured choices. Mostly I gave them recent past year exams from other Singapore schools. I planned their work schedule and checked in every weekend to see if everything was done, and done well. At this stage, I was still refining study skills. I wanted to see careful work, good handwriting... I was less fussy about grades than I was about general work quality. I threw absolute hissy fits when work was shoddy and careless, but looked past genuine errors and absolute scores.

At the end of Primary 3, Little Boy topped the class in Science. He certainly didn't expect it. When the Teacher announced the news, he looked dazed. His classmates didn't expect it because he had been such an underdog. They all spontaneously clapped for him. His self-efficacy for Science became a strong and robust component of his psyche.

But he was worried about Math.

Soon after, at the start of Primary 4, he topped the class in Math too. Again, his friends were so surprised that they applauded for him. So there it was. His self-efficacy for

Math was somewhat in place too.

More importantly, Little Boy began to believe that nothing was impossible. He seriously thought that he had done the impossible. I knew better. It was nothing that consistent practice and hard work could not achieve. Yet what matters is not what I knew but what Little Boy began to believe. He began to believe that what looks to be impossible, might not be so.

This gave him the courage to try and conquer Chinese by himself. I didn't make it easy. I took away his crutch - Grandma. I told him that swim or drown, he was on his own. He panicked not at all.

I asked him to memorise Chinese compositions. He had to spend 3 days a week of his December holidays, memorising Chinese 6 to 7 hours a day. He could not recognise more than half of the words in the first composition. The whole book had 1000 compositions of the same difficulty, some worse. He flinched not at all. He willingly put in the effort because he now believed that impossible was a state of the mind.

Primary 5: School Addiction

In addition, the intense rush of energy that came from a seemingly random, intermittent and variable top-of-the-class experience (for an explanation, track back to Chapter 7 on RIVR) kept him yearning for more. By Primary 5, Little Boy had become a school addict. School was able to give him a high. He wanted to experience the high again. And like a mahjong addict playing mahjong marathons, Little Boy went on a Chinese Compo memorising marathon. He wanted to top the class again, and he knew that his poor Chinese was standing in his way. He was a boy on a mission to fix his Chinese, just so that he could get another high from school.

Challenge 8.3:   *When Children Give Up*

Faced with failure, any normal child will want to give up.

The important thing is to help the child persist in the face of possible/actual failure from young. Parents who don't already master the strategies in earlier chapters, should not try this strategy as yet. To help keep the child on task when failure is highly possible, a parent needs the other motivational strategies documented in this book. For example, you would need to top up motivational energy through Emotional Connection. You need to know how to analyse Process. You need to know how to give Informational Feedback.

Challenge 8.4:   *Parents Live Their Children's Lives*

It is the rare person who doesn't feel good when he is able to influence his child towards desirable outcomes. To a greater or lesser extent, some part of us enjoys helping another – what more our child. Parents feel good when they help their children achieve. Parents share in the achievement too. It is the rare person who can steel himself enough to allow the child to own his victory by allowing the child to walk the Precipice of Failure. So much of our own ego is wrapped up in our children's success and failure, that when they do fail, we get hurt too. Many times, in the journey with my children, I tell myself that even if

they fail, I will still be proud of me and of them for having tried. I refuse to allow my children's failures to hurt my ego. That helps me to back off and allow them to taste failure in situations where I know there are no serious consequences. In situations where the stakes are very high, I will help... but there are many other occasions in 6 years of primary school where failure is relatively safe.

How To Provide Difficult Victories™

1. *See the difficulty of the task from the child's perspective.* The parent needs to make a judgment call. Can this task be conquered if I wait long enough? You can wait 3 days for a 9-month-old to put on his own shorts, it won't happen. On the other hand, there are parents who are still helping their five-year-old children dress themselves. Choose tasks that are a stretch for their developmental age. Expect of your child a little more than what you know he can comfortably achieve. To do this, you need to know your child.

2. *Help enough but not so much that your child thinks it isn't him.* Again, this is a judgment call. In an earlier family anecdote, I recounted how I introduced practice

exercises from Primary 3 onwards and how these practice exercises helped my children do much better in Primary 3 and Primary 4 than in the earlier years. The thing is, even though I helped by introducing practices, I still required that they manage their own practice schedule. They were also responsible for marking accurately. They had to brief me on the lessons they drew from the mistakes they had made. They put in more effort and time than I did. If the parent is putting in more effort than the child, there is something wrong when it comes to child motivation because the parent is more motivated than the child.

3. *Set your child up for success.* With a bit of planning, it is possible to control situations such that the child succeeds at something really difficult, and thinks he did it by himself. The next family anecdote illustrates.

THE BIG NEEDLE

The doctor's clinic had wide open doors. We passed it every time we went to the park to play ball. My children knew where the doctor's clinic was and what it looked like because I would point out the different shops on our way to the park.

On the morning of the vaccination, I took Little Boy on my lap and explained "Today, Mommy is going to bring you to the doctor's clinic to get your injection. We will first go and wait outside the doctor's clinic. After that, a very big man will use an injection needle to poke your bum-bum right here... or here... or here. It will be painful. A little bit like this (and I pinched Little Boy a little hard but not very). Now, you are a big boy and must not cry. If you don't cry, Mommy will be very proud of you. You will be a very good boy if you don't cry."

Once at the clinic, I made sure I pointed out the sequence of things that we had talked about earlier, so that my son could feel secure that things were going as planned. I also made sure that I was myself relaxed and calm because children pick up parental fear easily. When we got to the point where the doctor was preparing the needle, I talked about what the doctor was doing, and pointed to the needle. Then, I cuddled my Little Boy and said "Now, the doctor will give you an injection here. It will be painful, but Mommy will hold you tight, tight, and put plaster ok? You mustn't cry, ok? You are a good boy. I know you are a very good boy."

Very quickly, the doctor did his deed. Little Boy was taken aback by the pain but he did not cry. Then it was celebration time. Lots of kisses and praises about his amazing courage. The doctor of course was quite sincerely amazed at my son's performance and readily joined in the ooh-ing and ah-ing. How rare! How wonderful! It was a difficult victory well conquered, and properly celebrated.

For weeks after, all of us colluded to marvel at Little Boy's incredible courage, and ability to take pain. Little Boy strutted into his next vaccination appointment like a Warrior King in Pampers.

Many years later, Little Boy fell and a chunk of his ear came off. He didn't cry.

Firstly, it is extremely rare that babies not cry when being injected. I was injected as an adult and I cried a little. Secondly, notice how I was the one who controlled the event tightly in order to ensure that Little Boy didn't cry. I went to the extent of choosing an experienced doctor who wouldn't have to poke my son more than once. However, Little Boy was the one who took the credit for not crying. Even babies can experience Difficult Victories™ if parents take the trouble to set them up for success. In essence, you need to make a concerted effort to plan and set up a chain of events most likely to lead to the baby's success. After all the effort that you put in, you then step back and let the baby take the credit. Much later, in primary school, you should let the child work a bit harder for his success because by that age, they will be old enough to discern that they did nothing to earn the victory if you help too much.

4. *It is important to prevent your child from giving up*

along the way. Once he gives up, there is no difficult victory to be had. This can be done using all the motivational techniques already described

- ♀ Give structured choices
- ♀ Emotional connection
- ♀ Focus on process, not grades
- ♀ Give informational feedback
- ♀ RIVR (Please note that RIVP is not in this list. Technically, RIVP is used to discourage unwanted behaviour, not motivate desired behaviour).

5. When you help your child experience Difficult Victories™, there will certainly be failures along the way. A difficult victory would not be difficult unless there were some interim failures along the way. My children did not start by hitting the 90s in every subject. They worked up to it. They failed to hit the 90s many times. Before the hits, there were too many misses to count. *Failure management is therefore critical when helping children experience Difficult Victories™.* Failure management is a big topic and deserves the next chapter all to itself.

Failure Management: Learning Goal Orientation

Inspired by the work of Professor Carol Dweck and Professor Don Vandewalle.

WHAT IS LEARNING GOAL ORIENTATION?

Research documents 3 types of goal orientation[13]. These are:

- Proving goal orientation: The psychological focus is on proving that one can achieve the goal.
- Avoiding goal orientation: The psychological focus is on avoiding failure.
- Learning goal orientation: The psychological focus is on learning.

Students with avoiding goal orientation (i.e., who fear failure so much that they spend their entire school career trying to avoid it), generate very little enthusiasm/energy for school. When enthusiasm or energy is lacking, people give up.

Students with the proving goal orientation (i.e., who are out to prove they can) have a great deal of energy and enthusiasm for school right up till the moment they meet failure. The moment they meet failure, they have also proven to themselves that they cannot do it. Henceforth, such students believe that there is no point trying harder. It cannot be done. They had tried and failed. Therefore, they stop trying.

Students with the learning goal orientation (who are in school to learn) generate energy and enthusiasm from the lessons learnt from failure. Every new lesson learnt seems to give them more hope. With greater hope, is greater motivation. These students don't give up easily.

Why is Learning Goal Orientation Important?

A child equipped with a learning goal orientation sees the silver lining in every cloud of failure. He can summon energy to persist and overcome one difficulty after another because each difficulty teaches lessons. This child is as good as a car that uses garbage as fuel. This child takes every failure and comes back stronger, like the 9-headed Hydra from Greek mythology, which grew back 2 heads

for every head chopped off. A child that has a learning goal orientation grows in wisdom and strength every time he falls down. A child with learning goal orientation, who falls down enough, can become undefeatable. Such was the story of Genghis Khan.

GENGHIS KHAN, THE LOSER

Many people think of Genghis Khan as a bloodthirsty warrior who killed more people than anyone else in the history of mankind. Others think of Genghis Khan as a great ruler who built an empire of a size like none other. Genghis Khan's empire stretched from the Pacific Ocean (i.e., the waters around Japan) to the Mediterranean Sea (i.e., the waters around Turkey and Italy). However you look at it, history records Genghis Khan as a winner. Unlike Julius Caesar or Alexander the Great, Genghis Khan was not assassinated young. Even at death, he was a winner for he died at a ripe old age, in the care of a loving wife and whilst his empire was still expanding.

Few know that Genghis Khan's mother

described her child as a little boy who loved to cry and who was afraid of dogs. History records, but fails to emphasise the many failures of his youth. In his teens, he was constantly upstaged and bullied by an older half-brother. For a time, he was captured by another tribe and enslaved with a collar placed around his neck. Later, someone came by and kidnapped his wife.

However, Genghis Khan had a strong learning goal orientation. This is obvious from the way he is said to have learnt from enemies and friends alike. He was known to accept counsel. The Mongolians were illiterate but Genghis Khan adopted the Uighur script for his people. Growing up a nomad on the steppes of Mongolia, Genghis Khan knew little about city and empire administration. He listened to the advice of the peoples he conquered (i.e., his enemies) and learnt from them how to administrate, and then he improved on what he was taught. Indeed, in the time of the Khans, China was considered one of the safest countries in the world for merchants. In his book, "The Secret History of the Mongol Queens", Jack Weatherford wrote, "Bureaucrats sketched detailed portraits of all entering foreigners so that their pictures could be quickly circulated if they committed a crime. At each stop, the merchant had to register with the police, and his name was forwarded to authorities at the next stop before he could leave."[14] Clearly, Genghis Khan never allowed failures to tell him that he had proved he couldn't succeed at something (i.e., no proving orientation). Clearly too, Genghis Khan wasn't afraid to fail because he wasn't afraid of trying new things. He just went ahead to fail, and learn – learning goal orientation. Definitely!!

Indeed, he learnt constantly from the best warriors of other tribes every time he fought, whether he won or lost. He was a learner, and every time he failed he came back stronger. He was able to squeeze so much learning from every defeat that he soon became undefeatable on the Mongolian steppes and beyond.

When he first laid siege to a fortified city, he lost too. He was defeated in Western Xia (or Xi Xia) at the start of his military campaigns in that region. But he learnt and came back in 6 rounds of campaigns before he finally conquered Western Xia. From then on, fortified cities presented no problems because he had already learnt from 6 failures, and refined his battle tactics to deal with fortified cities. Thenceforth, nothing could stand in the way of Genghis Khan.

THE CHALLENGES OF CULTIVATING LEARNING GOAL ORIENTATION

Challenge 9.1: *Emotional Response*

When the child fails to meet expectations, parents can sometimes become more emotionally overwrought than the child. When this happens, it becomes difficult for the parent to sit down with the child to calmly review learning points from the failure. It helps to tell oneself that failure is never forever. Nobody except a drug courier caught at the

Singapore customs makes mistakes with lasting consequences that brook no remedial action. It also helps to tell oneself that if a parent does not quickly pull himself together and focus on learning from the failure, the next failure will be well on its way soon, because the lessons to avoid it were not properly learnt.

Look ahead, not behind.

Challenge 9.2:   *The Holier Than Thou Attitude*

It is also tempting to lecture the child on learning points. This only means that it is the parent who has learning goal orientation. This is no use. You need the child to have a learning goal orientation. It is better to ask the child to think through what he has learnt and what he intends to do. Then, give suggestions. This ensures that the child is himself primed towards a learning goal orientation. Be your child's friend in his hour of failure. Put him on your lap or hold him in your arms, and say kindly, "Tell Mommy what you have learnt from this experience?" Your comforting presence will give your child strength to face his failure, and soon you will be having a nice discussion on the lessons learnt for the future. Over many such discussions, your child will learn to face failure and learn from it.

The important thing is whether the child himself has learning goal orientation or not. If the child does not have learning goal orientation, but the parent does, then the child will simply move step by step as an automaton would, doing nothing more than what the parent desires.

HOW TO CULTIVATE LEARNING GOAL ORIENTATION

1. *As long as study process management was diligent and disciplined, console the child and encourage him to analyse his mistakes and plan ways to avoid them.* This may require study process redesign.

2. *If the process management was undisciplined and not diligent, reiterate the need to be disciplined and diligent.* As long as the child is small and may be forgiven for being clumsy, then this lesson can be gentle because the poor grade is already hurtful enough.

3. *Refrain from passing judgments about intelligence or personality.* Every child intuitively knows that he cannot do much about the IQ nor the personality he is born with. Such judgments hold a sense of finality and leads a child to say "I'm like that. Can't be helped. I give up." Instead, focus on what behaviours he can

change, do less of or do more of. Focus also on study process refinements e.g., more appropriate sets of practices or increased frequency etc… I used the following story to help The Daughter develop learning goal orientation.

A SQUIRREL'S NUTS

You know, darling, Life (with a capital "L") dishes out failures and successes in equal measure to everyone. It doesn't matter how smart you are, life is unpredictable and unfair. Those who eventually succeed in Life are those who can pick themselves up and carry on.

Mommy and Daddy cannot change the way the school teaches you and sets exams for you and marks your paper, in the same way that Mommy and Daddy cannot protect you from Life, with a capital "L". And even if we could, we may not want to. You need to learn to cope with Life, and the earlier you start, the better.

The only way to make failure into a good

thing is to learn from it. So what we would like you to do is to collect learning points the way a squirrel collects nuts. Every time you fail, you are to squeeze as many nuts out of the failure as you can. At the end of 4 years, you will have a whole mountain of nuts each representing a lesson learnt. You will be smarter, wiser and a much better person than you are today. And the more nuts you collect, the less you will fail in future.

10

Design the Self-Concept™

Inspired by the work of Professor Carl Ransom Rogers and Professor Joachim Tiedemann.

WHAT IS SELF-CONCEPT?

Self-concept is your concept of yourself. If you were asked to visualise yourself as a separate person, what do you see in your mind's eye? How would you describe the YOU in your mind's eye? What qualities does that YOU have? What faults? How would you describe YOU to yourself? Clever or stupid? Responsible or irresponsible? Adorable or irritating? Good or naughty?

WHY IS DESIGNING THE SELF-CONCEPT IMPORTANT?

Research shows that people tend to behave in a manner consistent with their self-concept[15]. If a child who thinks of himself as a "good boy", does something that turns out to be naughty, he experiences cognitive dissonance. Cognitive dissonance is defined as a feeling of "tension that arises when one is simultaneously aware of 2 inconsistent cognitions (i.e., thoughts or beliefs) [16]." For example, if you believe that you are neither a cruel nor violent person (a belief), and you realise that you have just killed someone in anger (a thought), the contradiction between your belief and your thought will stimulate very unpleasant feelings in you. These can be feelings of guilt for having done something you believed to be wrong. They can also be feelings of disgust at the realisation that you actually are the monster that you thought you were not.

It is the psyche's natural tendency to avoid cognitive dissonance as much as possible by behaving in a manner consistent with its self-concept. Therefore, if you don't wish that your child be irresponsible, undisciplined and lazy, then don't design these features into your child's self-concept.

Designing a positive self-concept in children is very important because some motivation researchers believe that it is difficult to change the self-concept once it has been established[17], and the self-concept is such a strong determinant of behaviour that parents really cannot afford to ignore it when developing internal drive in their children. If you want internally driven and achievement-oriented children, design that into their self-concept.

CHALLENGES OF DESIGNING THE SELF-CONCEPT

Challenge 10.1:   *Carelessness with Words*

Words have more power than we think. I guess that is why the phrase "The pen is mightier than the sword" was coined. Language can shape our reality. You need only look at the power of rumours (or even cyber bullying) to know how true this is. Every rumour contains a grain of truth and a lot of untruth. Spread that rumour far enough and even historical facts may be distorted. Words have power over your child's psychology, specifically when it comes to the child's self-concept.

Parents can sometimes be careless. I have seen some parents wag their fingers at their children affectionately and say "You are a naughty boy." It was meant to be affectionate and not serious, but a child does not know that. A child's psychology understands things very literally. The playful word "naughty" has more power over the child than we realise. This is a little bit like holding a mirror up to a child and playfully using a marker pen to draw little horns on the child's reflection on the mirror. The child who has never before seen his own mirror reflection understands the horns very literally as an integral part of himself. In the next family anecdote, I will show how a label can design a child's self-concept, and how that self-concept in turn determines behaviours.

THE HUMANITIES PROGRAMME

In Secondary 3, The Daughter was selected to enter a special class called the Humanities Programme. As the name suggests, the Humanities Programme offers an advanced curriculum in the Humanities subjects such as Literature, History and Geography. Collectively, the class was known as the "HP Girls", with an emphasis on the "H" for "Humanities".

Thanks to this label, the girls saw themselves as good at the Humanities and bad at Math. "That's why we're called HP, you see. We're not supposed to be any good in Math", they explained to their Teachers when the exam results at the end of Secondary 3 were analysed. The HP Girls had collectively managed to rank last of all the classes in Math.

The Teachers couldn't make sense of it because to make it into the Humanities Programme in the first place, the girls had to be good in Math too. When they were picked from the Secondary 2 cohort, the individual girls were at the top of their respective classes – or close. The poor Math Teacher for that class that year must have gotten a heart attack because a class of talented girls had dropped all the way to the bottom in Math. What's more, the Math teacher was one of the best the school had, and a terribly conscientious one too!!

In early Secondary 4, the Form Teacher went in guns-a-firing at the notion that Humanities students are not supposed to be good at Math. He showed them the analysis of their Math results in Secondary 2 and Secondary 3. He confronted them with the flaw in their logic with incontrovertible evidence, and asked a question the girls had no answer to. "How come all of you did well in Math in Secondary 2, if you're all supposed to be Math Idiots?!" he boomed from the height of his small head on wide shoulders and a beefy body.

The Math scores at the end of Secondary 4 went back up to where they were supposed to be. You see, people behave in a manner consistent with their self-concept. Hence, be wary of the labels you or others attach to your child.

Challenge 10.2:   *See What You Most Fear*

Designing the Self-Concept can also be challenging when parents fear certain traits of themselves (or of others). This predisposes them to latch on to some small random behaviour on the part of their children, and see in them the traits they most fear. The parents' hearts become fearful, and then, from the fullness of their hearts, their mouths speak negative words that sculpt the children's self-concepts more powerfully than they know. "You are lazy!!" "You are playful!!" You are stupid!!" In small children, the self-concept is unformed. Parents can choose consciously to

give it the shape that they most desire, or they can see things in their child that they fear, and comment on it often enough to successfully sculpt the negative trait into the child's self-concept.

It's a little bit like riding a bike and trying not to crash into a tree. You're so frightened of crashing into a tree that you keep your eyes locked on that tree. All you see is that awful tree, and when your eyes lock on to something, the rest of the body follows very naturally. And then what happens? You crash into the tree you were trying to avoid. So, when I was teaching my son to cycle, I told him "Don't look at the tree. Look at the road you want to ride on." In other words, don't look at what you don't want. Look at what you want.

In the same vein, I am telling parents "Don't look at the negative traits because you WILL see them in some random behaviour by your child. Focus your vision on the positive traits you want your child to develop." In the next family anecdote, I will show you how this can be done.

THE GIRL IS NO GOOD AT MATH

I started reading to The Daughter ever since she was 9 months old. I liked reading and she liked being read to. By the time she was 1 and half years old, she could trick people into thinking that she could read simply because she had memorised every word of her favourite stories, and knew exactly when to turn the pages. Not surprisingly, she learnt to read early and read voraciously.

When The Daughter came to lower primary, it fell to me to explain some mathematical operations to her. I am a certified Math Idiot. I didn't know how to explain properly. I blew up. The Daughter broke down.

It is often thought that those who are good at languages can't be good at Math, and vice versa. This widely held opinion, together with having witnessed the big blow-up between The Daughter and I over Math one night, lead Grandma to conclude upon her worst fears, "She'll never be any good at Math". In the weeks that followed, our naturally sociable and talkative Grandma told the all and sundry that The Daughter would always be better at languages than at Math. Often, this message was delivered within the hearing of The Daughter. There is so much finality in the word "never be good at something" don't you think?

I knew myself and was aware that if the Math session had ended in tears, it was very much my own incompetence at explaining simple Math. Added to that, my job at that time was quite stressful and I just didn't have the patience or the time to explain properly. I rejected this "math idiot" picture of The Daughter completely and thoroughly. That was not how I saw my little girl and I was certainly not going to teach her to see herself that way.

I took my daughter aside and told her that I was a Math Idiot, not her. And that I absolutely knew that she was far more gifted at Math than I. Then, I went on a propaganda offensive. I repeated to the all and sundry that I was an idiot mother with a gifted daughter.

Fast-forward a decade later. Throughout

her years in the Integrated Programme (which offers a very challenging Math syllabus), Math has never posed a problem to The Daughter.

How to Design the Self-Concept™

1. The story above shows

   ♀ How **ONE** event can be used to support an adult's judgment of a child (i.e., this girl will never be good at Math).

   ♀ How this judgment is then so often repeated in the hearing of a child that it eventually becomes a part of who the child thinks she is – "I am a Math Idiot".

   ♀ Before you know it, the child is behaving in a manner that is consistent with the initial judgment (which was itself only backed by **ONE** event) – She does poorly in Math.

   ♀ Then, the adult who first passed the judgment will say "You see! I was right! My clairvoyant wisdom and experience have read the child right."

   Actually, it had nothing to do with clairvoyance. It's just a case of a self-fulfilling prophecy. *Little children tend to become the person you say they are. So, if you don't want a naughty/stupid/irresponsible/irritating child, then try not to describe your child with such words.*

2. However, the truth is that children do naughty things in their ignorance. Children make stupid mistakes because they don't know better. Children irritate parents with shrieks and imitation fire engine sirens and constant kicking on the back of the passenger car seat! So how does one condemn these behaviours without condemning the child? *You could try to separate the naughty act from the child's self-concept.* One could say, for example "Pouring oat meal into the aquarium is an unkind thing to do to the fishes. Their gills will get clogged up and they will die of suffocation. You're a kind child, how did it happen?" or "These loud shrieks are irritating. You're normally a quiet kid, what's with you?" These comments condemn the act whilst affirming the child's positive self-concept. The act is naughty, but the child is good... oh so very good. And because the child believes he is good, he will ensure that he never repeats the naughty act.

3. *However, words are not enough to protect or to design our children's self-concept. Our children go through*

failure experiences in school that help our children to conclude that they are incompetent. Failing in school, getting scolded by teachers, losing to friends are all failure experiences that could get our children to think of themselves as losers. The Singapore school system is so competitive that if we are not careful, the system will design the notion of "loser" into our children's self-concept. In the next family anecdote, I will describe how obtaining mediocre results in Lower Primary convinced Little Boy that he wasn't "one of the smart ones" and how I successfully re-designed that portion of his self-concept.

I'M NOT "ONE OF THE SMART ONES"

When Little Boy was in Primary 1, I left him pretty much alone. His results were nothing to shout about. In the mid-year exams of Primary 2, his class placement dropped further.

In Primary 3, his class placement dropped even further. I discussed the matter with him. He said, "I am not the type to get good marks, Mommy. I am not the smart kind." Being the younger child who had gotten used to losing out to the older sister, my son possessed relatively lower self-efficacy (see Chapter 8 for a detailed definition of self-efficacy). He resigned himself very easily to failure that he thought inevitable. In this case, he seemed quite convinced that there was nothing he could do to improve his marks because he "was not the smart kind".

I pooh-poohed his suggestion and told him that it had nothing to do with smart or not smart. I said "Bad results usually come when a person has not worked hard enough. You are normally a responsible and hardworking boy, what happened? Will you work harder now?" Solemnly, he nodded his head.

That weekend, we went out to buy our very first Math assessment book. It was written by Andrew Er. We agreed that he would complete 4 problem sums every morning before he went to school in the afternoon. In the 3 weeks leading up to CA2, he completed small sections of previous years' math exams set by other Singapore schools. He obtained 94.5% for Math in CA2, scoring the same marks as another little boy whom my son describes as "one of the smart ones". I will forever be grateful to Andrew Er's genius for writing Math assessment books. Little Boy was overjoyed. He couldn't believe that he had done so well. He was amazed that he had actually scored the same marks as "one of the smart ones".

At this point, we had another discussion. I made very clear to him that if he hadn't done well before, it was because he lacked the effort, and not that he "was not one of the smart ones". I also pointed out that he didn't lose marks because he didn't know how to do the paper. He lost marks because he had carelessly neglected to check his work. Then, I went on to say "But you are a responsible boy! Now that you know it is because of hard work, will you continue to work hard?" Still jubilant from his achievement, he happily nodded his head.

However, I didn't stop there. I was determined to design the notion "I have talent in mathematics" into my son's self-concept. As he solved sum after sum after sum from the Andrew Er's assessment book, there came the inevitable difficult question. A few times, he was able to figure out the sum faster than I. On one occasion, he and I argued. We then found that his method was correct and mine was wrong. Using this small fact, I came to a deliberate snap judgment, "Wow! Son! You have inherited your father's talent for Math. You are naturally good at it. You have a talent for Math." I repeated this judgment to the all and sundry, and often in the hearing of Little Boy.

The way I went on and on about Little Boy's Math talent to him, his father, his sister, Grandma, Grandpa, Uncles and Aunties, you would think he was Einstein. Of course I knew he wasn't but as long as Little Boy thought he was, he was motivated to keep trying to achieve what he believed an Einstein should achieve. And when one tries, one will naturally do better than if one tries not at all.

I had left Little Boy alone to grope around in Lower Primary. He ranked 28 out of 38. Sometime in Primary 4, however, he topped the class for Math.

Later, in Primary 5, in the weeks leading up to the mid-year exams, I was most depressed. The jump from Primary 4 to Primary 5 was unimaginably big. I am not one to get easily discouraged, but as Little Boy did one practice exam after another, and could not complete any of the papers within the given time, I despaired. I despaired enough to get onto the Kiasuparents Forum and pour out my heart to unknown netizens. Many forummers encouraged me but in the end, it was Little Boy who was the greatest source of encouragement. I commented "It is ok if you don't do well in Math in the Primary 5 mid-year exams." He replied, "What makes you think I won't do well Mommy? I can't do them now but if I practice enough, I will be able to do well. I am not that bad at Math you know."

I had succeeded so well in designing the notions of (1) Math talent and (2) diligence, as robust components of Little Boy's self-concept, that they gave him the internal drive to persist in the face of difficulties that discouraged even me.

4. The above story illustrates 2 important points. *Firstly, the same snap judgment, prophetic statement and self-fulfilling prophecy process can work for you as well as against you. It can work for you when you understand the psychological mechanisms that underlie it and use it wisely to design a positive self-concept for your child.* In this case,

- I used one event (i.e., his solution to the math problem was right whilst mine was wrong) to support my judgment that he had talent in math.
- I then went around repeating this positive judgment to anyone and everyone who cared to listen, mostly in the hearing of Little Boy.

5. *The snap judgment, prophetic statement and self-*

217

fulfilling prophecy process can work against you when you don't understand the psychological mechanisms that underlie it. Therefore, you carelessly allow your own worst fears to lead you into loud negative prophecies about your child. In an earlier family anecdote (entitled "This Girl Is No Good at Math"), I recounted how Grandma went about loudly labelling The Daughter as a Math Idiot. She had no ill intentions. It's just one of the things many people do without understanding the serious implications.

6. *The above story also shows that there is a difference between improve-able and immutable conditions.* Attributing a failure to a lack of effort, points to an improve-able condition. The next time, one can work harder. Similarly, attributing a failure to having forgotten to check work, points to an improve-able condition. The next time, I can recheck my work. Attributing a failure to a lack of intelligence, points to an immutable condition. How can I improve my intelligence? Am I not born with it? I go through great lengths to ensure that "stupidity" is not part of my child's self-concept. The moment the child thinks he is stupid, he will stop trying in school. This is true

regardless of your child's actual level of intelligence. The child intuitively knows he cannot fight his genes.

7. *The irony is that the less intelligent your child, the more hardworking he or she needs to be, to keep up.* The less intelligent the child is, the more drive he needs to do well in school. If your child does not possess genius IQ, it really is best to steer away from attributing failure to lack of intelligence. Instead, attribute failure to a lack of effort. Don't people always say that "Genius is 1% inspiration and 99% perspiration"? Well, a kid who thinks he is dumb won't perspire and therefore, he will never be a genius.

11 | Set Goals

Inspired by the work of Professor Edwin A. Locke and Professor Gary P. Latham.

WHAT IS A GOAL?

A goal is a specific statement of what you want to achieve. It needs to be specific, challenging but still doable.

WHY IS GOAL SETTING IMPORTANT?

Firstly, when you set a goal, you help the child to visualise what he is to achieve. Research from the 1960s until now, has found that people with goals perform better than those without[18]. Given the same amount of resources such as time and energy, the child with a specific goal to focus his effort on, will perform better than another with no goal at all.

Secondly, when a goal is achieved, the child also has a

221

specific focus or reason for which to feel good. This specific focus for feelings of joy/triumph/elation facilitates the development of an addiction to school. Simply, when you achieve a goal, you feel happy. These positive feelings are attributed to the specific goal. If the goal is school work-related or subject-related, then school work or subjects themselves become associated with good feelings. If the good feelings about a particular achieved goal are highly intense, the psyche naturally wants to recapture the experience through the same route (school work or subject work). Goals provide a focus for emotion.

Emotions are important in building an addiction to school work. It's a little bit like how a gambling addiction develops (as I described earlier in Chapter 7). One day, you walk into the casino and slot a single coin into the jackpot machine. An avalanche of coins pours out. You stare at the pile of gold and feel joy - pure and unadulterated joy. You have never felt bliss of such purity and strength. You have a whole bag of coins that you have not used, and an avalanche of coins lying at your feet. You continue to feed the machine coin after coin after coin with the goal of hitting another jackpot. You hope... oh... you hope that there will be another avalanche. And then, randomly, it happens again. And you get another blissful high. Before you know it, you will be pulling that jackpot lever compulsively in the hope that the next one will be an avalanche. You pull and you pull and you pull.... There is nothing. Undeterred, you keep on pulling the lever and putting in coins. Hitting the jackpot was the specific event that caused you bliss. You are now addicted to the goal of hitting the jackpot because you experienced a high from it, and hope to, again. Gambling addicts are extraordinarily perseverant. They never give up no matter how much money they lose. In the next family anecdote, I will illustrate how the random scholastic goal achievement (bringing with it immense joy) can develop extraordinary persistence in your child in school.

PERSISTENCE IN THE FACE OF FAILURE

Truthfully, the first 4 months of Little Boy's Primary 5 came as a shock to me. As per our normal process, I covered all the new topics with Little Boy. By the time we were done, it was already 7 weeks before the mid-year exams. It was time to do practice exams so that Little Boy could develop a sense of timing for his exam paper.

Inexplicably, despite having mastered all the topics, Little Boy was barely passing the Math papers he practiced on. This was strange! Little Boy had never scored less than 80 marks even at his poorest practice exams in Primary 4.

Helpful parents on the kiasuparents forum advised me that this was quite normal for children in Primary 5. The reason is that even in the mid-year exam of Primary 5, schools were already setting papers of PSLE difficulty levels. This is to give children and parents a sense of what the children will face in 1.5 years time. In essence, the Primary 5 mid-year exam paper was too difficult for Little Boy by 1.5 years. No doubt, some topics to be tested in the PSLE were missing from the Primary 5 mid-year exam. However, for the topics that had been covered, the Math questions were of a complexity and sophistication that one expected only 1.5 years later.

We were all caught off guard.

The goal that we had set in Primary 4 was to score more than 90 marks for every practice math exam. I revised this goal down to 80. This was highly difficult but doable. On the 7th practice, Little Boy hit 80 marks. He was overjoyed. We were both pleased indeed. I celebrated his victory with him and we took a break for the rest of the day. He had been working so very hard. I felt for him, and I felt bad. I had visions of my son chained to his study table in the same way I had seen pictures of little 3 year olds chained to a post by the ankle in a brick kiln.

What's the difference? A little slave to making bricks, and a little slave to score 'A' in Math?

Right after, for the 8th practice, his marks dipped to 67. Little Boy went right back to work. He had this look on his face that said that he was going to keep at it until he hit jackpot again – 80 marks. Why? That was the specific stated goal, and getting to it made

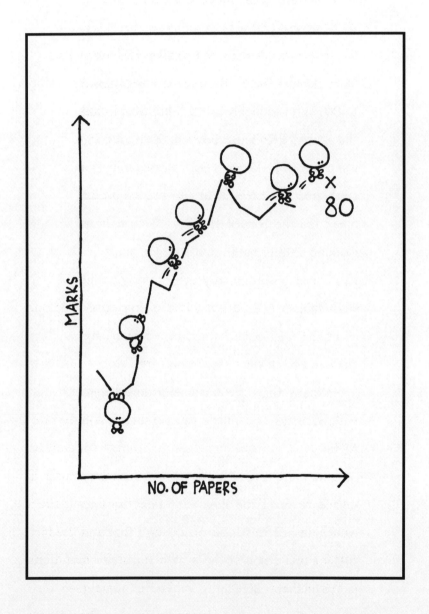

him happy. He had done it before and he could do it again.

Humans can be remarkably persistent in their search of an elusive happiness... especially if getting to that thing which gives the happy feeling is highly difficult but still doable. A goal is a focal point for effort and for feeling a sense of achievement. It goes some way in helping a child get addicted to school.

A third reason it is important to set goals is that one particular type of goals is very important to the development of a never-say-die attitude towards studying and living – impossible goals. Anyone who has succeeded a few times at doing something he thought he couldn't do, learns to look at the notion of impossibility differently. Rightly or wrongly, such people believe that nothing is impossible. And because this belief is deeply ingrained in their psyches, these are people who don't flinch in the face of difficulty. I make it a point to watch out for situations that are perfect for setting impossible goals (see also Chapter 8 above for more on impossible goals). We will see what the perfect conditions for setting impossible goals are later in the chapter.

The Challenges of Goal Setting

Challenge 11.1:   *Calibrating Goal Difficulty*

The challenge with goal setting lies in calibrating the goal difficulty. This is difficult because most parents are not familiar with the syllabus and the content to be tested.

For example, we had originally set the goal of 90 marks and above for Little Boy in every exam. We then realised that to make both parents and children get onto their toes and work really hard in the 1.5 years leading up to the PSLE, schools set exams in Primary 5 that approximated the level of difficulty one expected to find only in the PSLE.

Once we realised this, we knew that we had to recalibrate the goal we had set for Little Boy. A goal of 90+ marks would have been unrealistic since he had not been pre-taught the skills that would be required to do well in the Primary 5 mid-year exams. We set a new goal of 80+ marks instead. However, we were still unsure about whether this goal was challenging enough to stretch his effort but not so difficult that he would be discouraged. The balance was hard to find and required some familiarity with the syllabus and the child's abilities.

Challenge 11.2: Temptation to Set Blanket Goals and Use Threats
Of course, some parents set blanket goals. Someone I knew was told that he needed to be in the top 3 of his class every time or get caned. Another was told that he was never to come home with anything less than 90 marks or get caned. It turns out that both frequently met the goals set for them because of sheer terror. This is a brute force method and lacks some finesse. At best, it causes the child much anguish. At worst, your child will never see you again once he is old enough to leave home.

It is tempting to set such goals because parents are busy people. It is so much easier to manage the child from a highly macro perspective using blanket goals and tying negative consequences to them. It takes more effort to examine each situation and tailor a suitable goal.

Challenge 11.3:   Choosing the Type of Goal to Set
Goal setting is also challenging in that there are three different types of goals:

1.   Challenging but realistic goals
2.   Impossible goals

3.   Too easy goals

Knowing when to set which type of goal is not easy. I will clarify in the next section of this book, when to use which type of goal.

WHEN & HOW TO SET WHAT TYPE OF GOALS

When & How to Set Participative, Challenging & Realistic Goals

All goals set have to be specific. The challenging and yet doable type of goal is the classic sort that gurus will invariably advise people to set. If in doubt, you probably want to set these types of goals because they apply to the majority of situations. Hence, these are the type of goals that you should be setting most of the time.

For such goals, you want a level of difficulty that the *child views* as both doable and requiring effort. Please note the emphasis on the words "child views". It is the perception of the child that is important, not the adult's. Adult and child must sit together and set these goals. This said, many children do not know how to evaluate skills explicitly. Adults must evaluate how the child perceives the difficulty of the goal from facial expression, body language, past performance and other situational cues. It is not enough just to ask the child.

The specificity of a goal focuses attention. The difficulty of the goal stimulates a greater intensity and duration of effort. The doable dimension of the goal ensures that the child does not give up because he thinks he can never achieve the goal no matter how hard he tries. Again, let us stress that it is the child's perception that matters here. Hence, these goals need to be set with the active and willing agreement of the child.

When & How to Set Too Easy Forced Goals

These goals are useful when you are working with an extremely discouraged or unmotivated child. This child has very little motivational energy for schoolwork. The same child may be full of enthusiasm and verve when playing with his cousins, but the moment you mention school, all the energy disappears and the child becomes a zombie.

In such cases, we use too easy goals for two reasons:

- The child has little motivational energy. Challenging goals require a fair amount of energy to power the intensity and duration of the effort required to achieve them. If a highly discouraged and unmotivated child is given challenging goals, he will run out of energy in no time… He will look

231

around for fun things to do that do make him feel energetic. In other words, this child will get distracted from his goal achievement, and slip off to play at the slightest opportunity. Sounds familiar?

☿ Easy goals are quickly achieved. These provide experiences of short-term success that are important in building up a store of motivational energy. Every time a child achieves a goal, motivational energy is produced. Achieving a goal gives joy. If the goal is challenging and requires a lot of effort to achieve, goal achievement brings a great rush of motivational energy. If the goal is easy and requires little effort and time to achieve, goal achievement gives a small rush of motivational energy. Big or small, motivational energy is motivational energy. A succession of too easy goals, when achieved, adds to the child's severely depleted stores of motivational energy.

If a child is only somewhat short of motivational energy, then one can sit with the child to set these goals. If a child is so severely depleted in motivational energy that he actually actively flees school work, then one has no choice. One has to force these too easy goals on the child, and then monitor the child closely. The aim is to help the child to quickly achieve the goals and thus to experience multiple small infusions of motivational energy from goal achievement. These multiple small infusions will add up and altogether, they will replenish the child's stores of motivational energy.

Until the child has replenished his stores of motivational energy, he would not be ready to willingly sit down and set goals with an adult in any meaningful way. If he is not ready to sit down and set goals with an adult in any meaningful way, then it is premature to set challenging goals.

In the next family anecdote, I will share how I imposed too easy goals to replenish Little Boy's levels of motivational energy.

I Hate Studying, Mom

I didn't pay much attention to Little Boy's schoolwork when he was in Primary 1 and Primary 2. Back then, he was Grandma's boy. Grandma was his primary caregiver and she had taken it upon herself to supervise his schoolwork. I was more than happy to leave it to her.

I decided to take an active role when we received his report book after his Primary 2 mid-year exam. His class ranking had dropped and his attitude was poor. I could tell that he was quite demoralised by Grandma's nagging and criticisms. Nothing he did was ever good enough. Her love and concern for him translated into a stream of constant feedback for improvement: "This is wrong", "You are too slow", "Your writing is bad" and so on. On a daily basis, she told him exactly what to do, when to do it and how; and then she criticised his efforts. He was feeling really uninterested in school and schoolwork. It had become a real drag. He wanted to please us. He wished he could do better. But it seemed quite impossible to him. He had come to the defeatist conclusion – "Mommy, I am not one of the smart ones." He was so demoralised that he felt like a loser. He hated studying.

If Little Boy had been a car, his engine would have been cold and his battery would have been flat. When your car won't start because the battery is flat, it is still possible to ignite the engine by getting someone to push the car whilst you turn the key and press the gas pedal. In a way, you force the car to move in order to ignite the engine's drive. I decided to force Little Boy to move in order to ignite his internal drive.

I tried to package my "forcing". Being forced to do something is unpleasant enough. I didn't have to be unpleasant about it. I announced my intention at dinner in gentle tones. But I was firm and insistent.

Then we went out together to buy our very first Math assessment book. I chose the book and showed it to him, and told him that they were challenging problems and that we would do them together.

Then came the hard work for me. Every day for 2 months, I generated a To Do List for him. It was an item list with a few sums of

Math, and one or two English exercises. This item list gave him a series of specific and easy goals to focus on. I didn't ask his opinion when assigning these goals. I just told him what they were. Then, at the same time each day, I made sure he sat down at his work table and completed all the work without interruption. This regular schedule had a stabilising effect on him. He knew what to expect each day. Once he had started his work, I allowed him to interrupt me to ask questions, but I would never interrupt him. This was a first step to getting him used to independent work.

Depending on the amount of homework he had that day, I adjusted the specific goals I gave him. I made sure that I set an amount of work that was easy to complete. I made sure that the practices were easy. To encourage him to focus and to work quickly, I told him "I will never add more work than planned. If you can finish whatever I ask of you, the rest of the time is for you to play." This incentivised him to focus, and to quickly complete his work.

Since the quantity of work was easily managed, he could derive triple satisfaction from achieving the daily small goals I set for him. Firstly, he had the satisfaction of achieving his goals. Secondly, he had the satisfaction of being able to play without feeling guilty. In his opinion, it was play time that he had earned because he had focused well and achieved his goals. Thirdly, I always showed him that I was pleased every time he achieved the small goals I gave him. I praised. I smiled. I hugged.

Slowly, as he developed competence, I gave him gradually harder practices but always in a quantity that could be easily managed. As the days went past, the test dates got nearer. As they got nearer, he accumulated more and more motivational energy from his own daily successes and my daily praises of him.

With practice, he developed confidence. He had put in a lot of consistent practice and encountered many difficult problems whilst practicing. He had successfully solved them all. Every time he conquered the problems, he experienced a sense of achievement, and grew in confidence. Both feelings fed his motivational energy. His battery was getting well and properly charged up.

Little Boy ended up with a score of 94.5% for Math. He had topped the class. He surprised himself, his classmates and his Teacher. When his mark was announced, his classmates were so surprised that they spontaneously stood up and clapped.

The above shows that even though we know that forced goals, punishment and reward are extrinsic motivators that reduce internal drive, there is still a place in every parent's repertoire of motivational strategies for such unpleasant motivators. These can be useful on the rare occasion when the *child's batteries are flat and need an external push start. In such cases, you force a too easy goal and help your child meet a series of these, with copious amounts of praise and encouragement, enough to build up bit by bit some little motivational energy.* You have to recharge the dead battery by forcing the car to move little by little.

Note however that even though I call these "forced goals," I am very gentle when imposing them. The child has no choice in the matter, but I don't have to be brutish when forcing a goal. Typically, I would say "Shall we do this, my love? I think it will be good to do this little bit." If there is some resistance, I would escalate the level of insistence, saying "Come, my love. Do this now for me ok?" If there is more resistance, I would say "Let's do this now together." So, you see how it starts very gently. I've never escalated the insistence too far upwards. For example, I've never told my kids to just do it, or to do it or else. I've said that to renovation contractors who try and pull the woolies over my eyes, but never to my kids except when they refuse to bathe.

Since my focus is to build internal drive in order that my children can study independently of me, I very rarely even use forced goals.

When & How to Set Impossible Goals
I have never forced challenging nor impossible goals on my

240

children. In the rare instances when I force a goal, it is always a too easy one. When a goal is challenging or impossible, it is only effective when a child willingly commits to it. This is the only way to ignite any amount of internal drive that will get the child anywhere close to achieving the challenging or impossible goal.

Setting an impossible goal requires the following:

1. An emotional connection of extraordinary bandwidth

2. Complete trust in the parent

3. A child with already a reasonable amount of motivational energy towards school work.

4. A parent on standby to provide Emotional Connection and Informational Feedback.

5. A child's willing commitment.

6. A very honest appraisal of the benefits and costs of achieving the goal.

In every instance where I have gained Little Boy's commitment to an impossible goal, he gave me his commitment without really knowing what the goal achievement journey would entail. Sometimes, even I myself didn't realise how difficult the goal really was. However, I always let him know that what we were about

to do was very difficult but if he was willing to try, I would help him. He gave his commitment to the goal because he was 100% sure that I would see him through to the end with Emotional Connection and Informational Feedback. Little Boy trusted me completely. Therefore, like a little Sam Gamgee following his master Frodo Baggins into Mordor (in the movie Lord of the Rings), my son followed me all the way to hell to achieve an impossible goal.

It is important to never lose the trust your child has in you because that means that your child will not follow you into hell again. The adult that proposes an impossible goal is as much invested in the goal as the child who has to achieve it. If my son fails at achieving the impossible goal, I will make sure I share the blame. If you leave your child alone to bear the failure, he will never trust you enough to follow you into Mordor again. This will make it very difficult to successfully inculcate the never-say-die attitude because your child will promptly give up at the first sign of an impossibility. As a result, your child will never experience conquering impossible goals.

Of course, by sharing the blame of failure with the child, it is not to say that we shield our children from what should be their accountability. If a child makes a decision

243

on his own, he is wholly responsible. However, if he makes a decision because of me, then I am partly responsible. I have thus to make sure I don't abandon him to any negative consequences that might ensue from a decision I encouraged him to make. I am invested too and so we will both bear the pain of failure together.

I have actually touched on impossible goals earlier in the section entitled Self-Efficacy: Difficult Victories™. The best kind of impossible goals to set, are those that look impossible but are imminently doable, given enough time and effort. In effect, they are doable goals in disguise. A good example of such an impossible goal was the one where Little Boy had to write out from memory, a 2000 word Chinese Model Composition. I didn't know how terribly hard this goal looked until a friend with a Diploma in Translation (Chinese-English) expressed her shock. It took Little Boy about 5 days (of 7 hours each) before he could successfully write out the whole composition from memory. However, close examination of such a goal shows that it really just needs time and consistent effort. Success is sure. However, your child does not see that. The goal looks impossible but it really isn't.

THE 2000 WORD CHINESE COMPOSITION

After the Primary 5 exams, Little Boy could learn to fluently read up to 4 Chinese Model Compositions (of between 1000 to 2000 words each) within 4 hours. This was in sharp contrast to the 7 hours he needed to learn up a single compo 10 months before. I proposed to him to push the envelope of his skills upwards by setting another ambitious goal – reproduce in writing and from memory, 5 Chinese Model Compositions. The first composition he tackled was a whopping 2000 words long. That alone took 6 days to master.

Of course, to write out 5 Chinese Model Compositions from memory, was a very challenging goal. Therefore, I needed his willing commitment. I let him know that I wasn't sure how useful the process would be. I explained that it would require a lot of effort, and might take very long. I needed his fully willing commitment so I had to provide full information too, including the bit that I too had incomplete information about what this would entail, and the results that may or may not come. He thought it over 2 days. He then decided to go ahead and give it a go.

It took 15 full days of hard work to be able to successfully write out from memory 5 Chinese Model Compositions. Along the way, I asked him a few times whether he was sure he wanted to complete the target 5 Chinese Model Compositions. By this time, Little Boy had experienced many, many Difficult Victories™ so he had a rock solid belief that it's all about trying hard enough. By this time too, a robust component of his self-concept included the notion "I am not a quitter." So, since he had properly considered the pros and cons of this new and very challenging goal, and had decided to commit to it, he wasn't about to quit. To help him along, I used Emotional Connection and Informational Feedback to feed him with regular doses of motivational energy.

Once he had achieved the goal, we evaluated the process, and guess what... we concluded that we had just wasted 3 precious weeks of the school holidays. The process gave us too little gains for too much effort. Oh well... we knew that nothing might come out of it when we started. So, we shrugged our shoulders and devised another process. Let's move on.

2 days later, Little Boy commented to me. "Mom, I don't think those 5 Chinese Model Compositions were a complete waste of time. When I started I wasn't sure if it could be done. The first composition was 2000 words long. How can anyone write that out from memory? But then I did it. I am now convinced that nothing is impossible if I have enough time to keep at it."

This came from the horse's mouth without prompting from me. I had never explained to Little Boy what it was I was trying to develop in him all these years – the never-say-die attitude. But here he was, summarising to me so precisely the end result of a very long term developmental strategy that I had

247

patiently enacted upon him since he was a baby, about to walk into the doctor's clinic for a painful injection.

12

Specify-and-Magnify

Inspired by the work of Jane M. Watkins and Bernard J. Mohr.

WHAT IS SPECIFY-AND-MAGNIFY?

Specify-and-Magnify, as a method, started in organisational consulting and research. Business consultants used Specify-and-Magnify to develop organisations. Specify-and-Magnify typically directs its attention toward positive events or positive examples found naturally (perhaps randomly) within work units and organisations. It then uses these events and examples as positive models[19]. Specify-and-Magnify is especially useful when employees have already been told many times about their "problems". However, they are at a loss as to how to solve them. Hence, they are feeling a great deal of negativity. The positive orientation of Specify-and-Magnify enables groups to overcome these negative tensions and make progress in the spirit of hope towards a positive future.

I adapted the method for my children, and here is how I define it for kids. Specify-and-Magnify directs its attention toward positive events or positive examples found naturally (perhaps randomly) in children's behaviours. It then highlights these positive behaviours and brings them to the attention of the child. Specify-and-Magnify is especially useful when children have been too often criticised and made aware of their "problems". However, children being children, they might know what is wrong (because adults tell them all the time), but they don't know how to fix themselves. They are at a loss as to how to fix themselves. The positive orientation of Specify-and-Magnify enables children to overcome these negative tensions and make progress in the spirit of hope towards a positive future. The following anecdote illustrates the definition of Specify-and-Magnify.

It is a much more motivating way of moulding behaviour than criticism and negative feedback. Focus on what the child has done right, and amplify it.

GOOD DEDUCTION SKILLS, BOY!!

One day, a Daddy brought his son to me because I offered to generate a motivation recipe for both parent and child to implement at home. We worked on getting the child to memorise a Chinese Model Composition wherein 50% of the words were alien to the child. The Daddy explained that his son could not focus, and was too playful.

I first worked one-to-one with the child whilst the Daddy observed. The child had very little motivational energy so I imposed a too easy goal. "Come... Sit down here. You memorise this one sentence for Auntie, ok?" Then I sat down and smiled at him as he began. With me by his side, he stayed on task. When he was done and could recite the single sentence to me, I commented him on his ability to focus, and his success at explaining difficult words to me clearly. I had thus picked up on 2 positive events in his performance and made them salient by commenting on them. By doing so, I was also telling him that

251

these were the behaviours I wanted.

Next, the Daddy worked with him. I became the observer. When it came to the point of recitation, the Daddy only commented when his son made a mistake in pronunciation. At one point, the Daddy asked his son to explain a word. The son made a gesture that sufficiently illustrated the word, but the Daddy wasn't attentive enough to pick up the gentle gesture and so the Daddy growled the translation of the word in English. It was very subtle, but I observed how the son shrank a little like he had just been caught in error.

In Specify-and-Magnify, you learn to ignore the mistakes and pick out the desirable behaviours or the good things the child has done. In every sequence of behaviours, there is good and bad. There are things the child gets right. There are things the child gets wrong. In Specify-and-Magnify, you ignore the bad and zoom in on the good. With each interaction between you and the child around a task, you keep picking out the good and amplifying it. The child will naturally respond to your approval by doing more of the good things that you've highlighted. Meanwhile, ignore all the bad… for the moment.

If the Daddy were enacting Specify-and-Magnify, he would have watched his son carefully to note even the slightest good behaviours. He would then have been able to pick out the small gesture his son made to illustrate a word. He could then have commented on it and said that it was a smart piece of deductive thinking. This would have communicated to his son that when reading a passage in Chinese, being able to deduce the meaning of unknown words is a desirable skill. This positive event becomes salient. Next, the Daddy could have picked up on the many words that his son did read correctly, and comment on the son's ability to recite accurately. Instead, the Daddy only responded to the three mistakes the son made in the whole sentence, and he brushed aside his son's laudable attempt at deducing meaning from context.

WHY IS SPECIFY-AND-MAGNIFY IMPORTANT?

I find Specify-and-Magnify useful because it teaches positively. There is no need to make mistakes to learn. When you do assessment books before you have actually mastered the material, you basically are trying to learn from every mistake you make. This can be very demoralising because each mistake is a negative event that costs you a little in terms of motivational energy. Specify-and-Magnify is the exact opposite of learning from assessment books. It allows me to mould behaviour using positive events. As one positive event after another is highlighted, motivational energy accumulates. Children begin to feel good about what they're doing. Here is another example of what Specify-and-Magnify is.

YUMMY VOCABULARY, SIMILES AND EXCITEMENT LEVELS

One of the things Teachers look for in PSLE English Compositions is well-chosen vocabulary. When Little Boy was in Primary 4,

As one positive event after another is highlighted,
motivational energy accumulates.

I pulled out a few blog posts from my blog (www.petunialee.blogspot.com) and showed him how this word and that word was both unusual (i.e., not commonly seen in less well-crafted writing) but well-chosen for the context. My specifications for vocabulary use were more fine-grained than merely stating "Use big words". I used a positive model to show him yummy vocabulary.

Then, Little Boy wrote something for me. I took a green pen and went through his writing, circling every single instance of yummy vocabulary I could find. I ignored the boring vocabulary. I did not try to replace the boring vocabulary therein with yummy vocabulary. All I did was to appreciate the yummy vocabulary he had put in there.

By chance, a simile had appeared in his writing. I underlined the simile – "The old man's face was as wrinkled as crinkled parchment", thus bringing it into salience. I stated that I wanted to see more of such similes in his writing. In his next composition,

I went through and circled both yummy vocabulary and similes. I gave not a single negative feedback and yet his composition writing was improving feature by feature.

Next, using the composition that he had already written, I sat down and plotted the excitement levels inherent in his story line simply from what he had already written. See Figure 12.1 below.

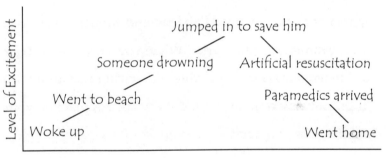

Figure 12.1   Excitement Levels

By bringing into salience the notion of excitement levels in his story line, I drew his attention to it. Then I commented that I really liked that the contrast between the excitement levels from one point of the story to the next. In his next compositions, I noticed that he took special care to further accentuate the difference in excitement words. His calmness words conveyed peace and tranquillity. His excitement words conveyed heightened danger and suspense. He was already writing more vividly without me having to criticise him even once.

THE CHALLENGES OF SPECIFY-AND-MAGNIFY

Challenge 12.1:   Lack of Patience

Impatience is the enemy of Specify-and-Magnify. Can you savour champagne in a hurry? When you've made up your mind to savour a meal at a Michelin-starred restaurant, do you gulp it down in 5 minutes? You can't appreciate your child if you're in a hurry.

Challenge 12.2:   The Know-It-All

Parents are supposed to know more. We expect ourselves to know more, and be better. Since we are supposed to be expert, we have a tendency to show off, to judge and to evaluate... more than appreciate. Having the attitude of someone who knows more, we become less sensitive to the things the child already can do without being overtly taught. Instead, we attempt to preach and teach what we should merely observe, pick out and encourage.

Challenge 12.3:   *Magnify What?*

Specify-and-Magnify works when you can recognise what is good. If you are not aware of the elements of good writing, you can't identify nor find the features of good writing to make salient. If you identify the wrong element, then you are encouraging the wrong thing. For example, I thought that creativity of storyline was desirable. I picked out creative storylines and commented on them. Little Boy's stories then got ever more fantastical. In Primary 6, we realised that Teachers marked compositions down when the story lines veered too far from what the markers expected. I was appreciating the wrong thing, and caused my son to do more of the wrong thing.

Challenge 12.4:   *Out of Control!*

Specify-and-Magnify can get out of control. Seriously out of control. I made it a point to develop Little Boy's sensitivity to study process improvements. I did this by constantly asking him what he thought of the study process I proposed. At first, he said he didn't know. After a while, he began to share how he felt about what he was doing for me e.g., "Mom, I think that instead of doing just 2 sums from each sub-topic, I should do all of the sums in this particular sub-topic" or "Mom, when I come home on Wednesdays, it is late. I prefer to do a 50 minute English composition practice instead of a 1 hour 40 minute Math paper."

I would pick up on his feedback and comment on it. For example, I said "It is good that you have developed a sense of what you need to do to master a topic. By all means do all the sums in this particular sub-topic." I also said "I agree with you. On Wednesdays, you're tired when you come home and you have little time to do a long Math paper. This is good planning." Little by little as I made salient what I specifically appreciated about each of Little Boy's suggestions to improve or refine his study process, he developed competence and confidence in his decisions about how he should study. Soon, he wanted to make his own decisions without my agreement. He became more insistent in what he thought he should or should not do.

Once, he insisted to work on Sundays. This was because I had often commented on his stamina and his willingness to do whatever it took to master a topic. I had often commented that he was not the sort of boy to take the easy way out. Make no mistake about it. Little Boy loves his Sundays because it is the only day where we do not schedule work. He loves playing, and I love to watch him play on Sundays with wild abandon. But in January of his PSLE year, he pushed me hard to allow him to do work on Sundays. His willingness to do whatever it took to master his work had gone quite overboard I thought. His insistence to follow a study process that he wanted was also a bit too strong. In the end, I vetoed his insistence without explanation because I knew we still had a good 8 months to go, and he was so motivated that he was doing very consistent work, and so we didn't need those silly Sundays. Besides, I could just imagine how tired he would be by the time the PSLE came around if he had to work 7 days a week, 10 hours a day, for 8 months. In the next anecdote, I will recount another example of how Specify-and-Magnify went out of control.

MA'AM I RENTED IT

I used to teach HR Consulting to undergraduate business school students. Undergraduate students being undergraduate students came dressed like students – in shorts, slippers, mini skirts, tank tops. However, one of the key basics in consulting, even before you get anywhere near knowledge transfer is presentation. My first boss in the consulting world explained, "You must look good, smell good and be on time."

I went to class dressed in a corporate suit and I explained to the students that self-presentation and personal branding was key in every industry and every office. Hence, as students about to graduate, they needed to don the ethos and sartorial habits of the corporate world. I then organised the students into project teams and gave out a project assignment for presentation next week.

When next week arrived, one of the groups contrived to come in office wear. I commended them for it and then publicly awarded bonus points for Professionalism. In that same week, another group put up very neat PowerPoint slides that were clear and readable. I picked up on that and commented that the slides were "elegant" and "engaging".

They weren't really fantastic slides, but they were all I had to comment on.

The week after, all five groups appeared in office wear. There were 2 or 3 individuals who looked out of place in rags, but I expected that these would sort themselves out in another week or 2. Every group came with nice slides. 2 groups came with really good slides. The animation, pictures and words came together to convey meaning. I would have been proud to present those slides myself to clients. Before long, the students were surpassing themselves from week to week. My general direction was that good presentation was valued. They noted features of their classmates' work and went one up each time on each other.

The project groups had to deliver a consulting assignment to a real client. A portion of their marks was a 30-minute presentation of their consulting report and findings to a panel of judges. I was of course, on that panel. I arrived at the lecture hall and immediately felt under-dressed. Many of the students were wearing suits. One student told me "Ma'am, I rented my suit especially for this presentation." I was so shocked and embarrassed I didn't know what to say. I felt a bit guilty that I had caused unnecessary expenses for this young man with not yet a job.

Specify-and-Magnify can go out of control. I haven't figured out how to stop it spinning out of control yet. If I do, I will write another book.

HOW TO SPECIFY-AND-MAGNIFY

1. Know exactly *what is good.* If you don't know what is good, you have to find out. Else, you can't use this strategy.

2. *Be very observant* so as to pick out positive events/behaviours.

3. Positive events and behaviours won't happen in any predictable order. *One must therefore be opportunistic. Watch. Wait.* Then, pounce on something you can specify into salience. In the many mornings when Little

Boy had to be woken up, I said nothing. One day, he did wake up when his alarm rang and got ready for school because I was ill with flu, and could not wake up. I commented on how amazing it was that a Primary 3 Little Boy had the self-discipline to wake himself up at 5.15 am in the morning. From then on, he tried to do that. He knew he could do that because he had done it once before. He knew I appreciated it too. That is the beauty of Specify-and-Magnify. Half the battle is won because you're working on behaviours that the child has already demonstrated. Therefore, the child knows that what you appreciate is well within his capability.

4. Specify-and-magnify is especially potent if the Emotional Connection between child and parent is very strong. The child knows that something pleases you. This pleasure comes through the emotional umbilical cord to him. This infusion of positive emotion is pleasant, and the child will try to experience the pleasure again. *If your Emotional Connection with your child is strong, several strategies in this book become more powerful.*

5. Sometimes, you might not get any really excellent event to comment on. For example, in the 2nd week of class

with my business school students, I didn't get really fabulous slides. I took what was good enough to be described as "somewhat elegant" and I said that it was "elegant". You don't have to wait for a truly elegant something to appear because it might not ever appear unless you first make the criteria salient. *Pick on something approximate, and magnify it.*

6. *You can provide a positive model.* I did that when I walked into class in a corporate suit to teach my business school students. I also did that when I pulled out my blogposts to help my son appreciate yummy vocabulary. What is better is to discern from the sequence of unschooled and untrained behaviours of your child those you can comment on and bring into salience.

7. *Ignore the negative.* The important thing in Specify-and-Magnify is to build on strengths. Once you have amplified enough strengths, you will already have some sort of good performance plus a lot of motivation. Once you have amplified enough of the positive (i.e., until there is nothing else to amplify) then you can begin to give negative feedback. However, when you use Specify-and-Magnify, and you are patient, you can

already accomplish a lot before you turn to negative feedback. Every child does many things in a day. Find those behaviours you like and appreciate them. The child will naturally try and enact other behaviours he thinks you will like. He's just trying his luck but it still means you have more to comment on. And you also can pull positive models from elsewhere to show to your child, provided that

- these are not positive models cited to incite competition and rivalry e.g., "Your sister is better than you are."

- these are not positive models cited to put down your child e.g., "I don't understand why you can't be like Mrs Tan's daughter. Look at her. She is perfect! Not like you."

13 | Physical Movement

Inspired by the work of Professor Stephen R. Marks.

WHAT IS PHYSICAL MOVEMENT?

This term is probably self-explanatory. Nonetheless, let us define it anyway. Physical movement refers to any movement you make with your body. This includes shaking a leg, twirling your pen, walking around, jogging or running up and down the stairs.

WHY IS PHYSICAL MOVEMENT IMPORTANT?

Physical movement raises heartbeat. When a woman is attracted to a man, her heartbeat goes up. When Little Boy sees a plate of pork carnitas, his heartbeat goes up. When I think of spending a Saturday morning gardening, my heartbeat goes up. When The Husband sits up in bed on

269

Sunday morning and thinks about his plan to DIY a water recycling system at home, his heartbeat goes up. A slightly raised heartbeat gives one a sense of vitality and energy[20]. This is why people feel more energetic after a jog. This is why regular exercise is sometimes recommended as part of depression treatment. Physical exercise is also known to stimulate the production of endorphins – the feel-good hormone. If you think of motivation as a feeling, then physical movement is an indispensable tool in the motivation toolbox. How so?

The human mind can be confused into believing that it likes something more than it actually does, when heartbeat is raised by physical activity. In a famous experiment on male-female attraction, psychologists Donald Dutton and Arthur Aron asked men to walk across a wobbly and narrow 450-foot-long bridge suspended 230 feet above the rapids of the rocky Capilano River[21]. To fall would be certain death. An attractive young woman met each of these men in the middle of the bridge and asked for help to fill out a questionnaire. She then gave the men her phone number and invited them to call her if they wanted to know more about her project. Most took the number. Half of these, called her. By contrast, men who were asked to cross a low, solid bridge rarely called. Men who were met by another man, in the middle of the suspension bridge, also rarely called. The heightened heartbeat that resulted from crossing a shaky suspension bridge high up above a dangerous looking river confused the men into thinking that they were very attracted to the girl in the middle of the bridge.

Now, I am not suggesting that you make your child do his Math homework in the middle of a dangerously wobbly bridge just to confuse his brain into thinking he likes Math. If he already hates Math, doing this will terrorise him even more, because fear and anxiety also come with heightened heartbeat. I hope you noticed that in Dutton and Aron's experiment, they did place an **ATTRACTIVE GIRL**, not an old hag. You want heightened heartbeat that is associated with a mildly positive or neutral experience, not heartbeat that comes with a negative experience – such as fear and anxiety. Fear does motivate in the short term, but you don't want to go there because negative heightened heartbeat emotions lead to burnout. Your child will avoid school, avoid learning and maybe avoid you. When old enough, you will lose connection with the child. When you do lose connection with your child, you are the ultimate loser.

I do suggest however, that parents consider using physical movement as a way to prevent the brain from falling asleep. Many of the activities associated with developing skill (and that includes thinking skills) are tedious. For example, mathematical ability in later life sits squarely upon a solid foundation of computational speed and accuracy. Computational speed and accuracy are like the strength and flexibility training that gymnasts need to build up in order to support the complex movements that go into a gymnastics floor routine. You can't do a flip without strong stomach muscles, nor can you manage the rings without good upper body strength. You can't do a split without flexibility training either.

To build computational speed and accuracy, it helps to practice loads of computations – 4-digit long division, long multiplication, long division, long addition and subtraction. Practice makes perfect, but practice is also tedious. For such activities, it helps to interrupt the practice session with some walking around.

RUN TO ME & RECITE

One of the most tedious things that Little Boy had to do was to memorise and recite Chinese

Model Compositions. This activity was so tedious that I required Little Boy to quickly run to me to recite his chunk before he forgot. What Little Boy didn't know was that I wanted him to run to get his heartbeat up. He thought I wanted him to run so that he could recite before he forgot. Very often, I would be upstairs, so Little Boy had to run up the stairs to get to me.

The period after lunch was particularly challenging. Little Boy likes his food and if you're engaged in an uber-boring activity like memorising compositions, lunch is a welcome respite and I made an effort to prepare yummy lunches that Little Boy would eat a lot of. The after-lunch sleepy syndrome was a challenge to manage. Often, I could see Little Boy yawning as he strove to stay on task. At such moments, I would initiate a wrestling game where I might try to bite his nose or get a finger poke at his soft, full belly. An hour after lunch, I might actually send him to the pool for a few laps. At other times, I would

get him to do a slow jog.

It is always tempting to send the child off for a nap but if the child has had a full night of good sleep, there is no reason to do that. That isn't the best way to wake the brain up from tedium. Naps are useful when the activity has been very challenging and has required multiple thinking skills and a high degree of concentration. In that case, the brain is truly tired and benefits from a rest. If the brain is tired from tedium, then physical movement is better to keep the brain sharp and alert.

CHALLENGES OF USING PHYSICAL MOVEMENT

Challenge 13.1:   *Knowing When*

There are some study activities that will be completely derailed if you interrupt the child's train of thought with imposed physical activity. For example, if your child is writing an English composition for you, then asking him to walk around after every sentence will be very frustrating because one sentence builds upon another, and when you lose your train of thought, you need to pick up the threads again before you can continue to write. Or, if your child is doing a Math problem sum, it wouldn't do to interrupt him after every line of working to ensure he gets enough physical activity to stay on task. You would be in fact, distracting him from task.

Challenge 13.2:   *Knowing How Much*

Slotting physical movement into a study process requires some attempt at knowing how much. Physical movement breaks the monotony of a tedious study process, enough to wake the brain up and bring it back on task. Nothing is being learnt as you engage in physical movement. Hence physical movement consumes time without actually teaching anything. Too much of it is a waste of time. Leaving a young child to manage the process alone may not be ideal. The physical activity break will be so fun (compared to the tedium of memorising compositions) that the child will get absorbed in it and waste time.

Physical movement is the only part of the study process that I don't try to completely delegate to Little Boy. If parents want to try delegating the management of physical movement to your children, you can. I just want to share that I have myself not tried it because I needed tight control of how much and when to maximise time use. Even if I do get Little Boy to help manage the insertion of physical movement into the study process, I ensure that I retain a major part of the control. For example, when getting him to recite chunks of a Chinese Model Composition, I defined that he needed to come and recite to me after every 6 lines. All Little Boy needed to do was to ensure he came to recite to me after memorising 6 lines. How long he would stay away from his desk was then controlled by me because I determined how far away from him I would place myself.

Depending on the situation, I might move myself downstairs and ask for a recitation after every 2 lines. This shortens the time he needs to stay at his desk, but it also shortens the distance he needs to walk to me. The greater the tedium I observe, the more frequent the interruptions I will introduce, but each interruption will be shorter (i.e., my distance from him is shorter).

HOW TO USE PHYSICAL MOVEMENT

1. *Evaluate the task carefully to ascertain that it is a series of repetitive acts that don't build on each other,* e.g., 20 different long division sums. You can interrupt the child after every 2 or 3 sums and not break any

277

coherent train of thought because each long division sum is independent of the others. The same applies to reciting a Chinese Model Composition chunk by chunk. Since I did not require him to recite the whole composition to me at one shot, each chunk was independent of the others.

2. *Watch the child carefully for tedium fatigue.* There is no sense in interrupting routinely after every 2 chunks/sums etc... If the child can still focus and shows no indication of tedium fatigue, let him continue through to 3 or 4 or 5 or even all 20 long division sums. This is a way of training focus and concentration.

3. *There is no need to tell your child what you're doing* (especially if like me, you have decided to keep the interruptions entirely under your own control). Just watch and observe for tedium fatigue and intervene appropriately. Calibrate the length and frequency of interruptions to the situation i.e., your child's energy levels that day, the weather, the time of the day etc... Till today, Little Boy doesn't know that there is method in my madness when I deliberately go upstairs to the 3rd storey of the house to wait for him to run up 2 flights of stairs to recite to me, and then run down

again 2 flights of stairs to memorise the next chunk. He also has no clue why I would suddenly initiate a tickle session or ask him to come help me plant some seeds.

4. *Be creative in your choice of interruptions.* Anything that gets the child moving is fair game here e.g., plant a seed, drink some water, throw a ball. My favourite games are tickle battles, chewy ear, bite the nose and deal with the pinchies. However, I'm game for anything that gets my child to laugh out loud and run around the house... for a short while.

5. *Be wise in your choice of interruptions.* Any interruption that is too long is a no-no e.g., go buy milk (20 minutes), bathe the dog (30 minutes). You can't afford to take the child away from his work after every 6 lines of recitation for 30 minutes. Not much work will be done then.

6. Chunk by chunk, sum by sum, interspersed by giggles and movement, the child will progress slowly through the task. Time will fly past and the task will be completed without the child falling asleep or losing focus. It was hard work but there was levity in the process. At the end of the long and arduous task, *use the opportunity to sculpt the child's self-concept* by

saying "I can't believe you actually memorised and recited this 2000 word composition to me. The task looked quite impossible even to me. You must be an extraordinarily persistent child."

14 | The Last Chapter

Inspired by all the mistakes I made.

BEWARE OF HIDDEN DANGERS

If you have read every page of this book till now, you would hopefully have achieved some understanding at least of 11 motivation strategies. You might consider them to be tools in your motivation toolbox.

The thing about tools is that their effectiveness depends on...

1. Whether you are using it for the appropriate situation, and

2. How skilfully you use the tool.

I have attempted to give rich illustrations using actual events and experiences in order to give readers a sense of the context in which each motivational strategy can be appropriately used. However, words can only communicate so much. In reality, life surrounds us with a richness that no amount of words can pin down. Hence, I am unsure that I have been exhaustive in describing the boundaries of effectiveness for each strategy (i.e., the situations most suitable for its use). I am also unsure whether I have exhaustively listed all the things to be careful of when using each strategy. Wrongly used, every strategy has the potential to damage your child. This is true of anything that has effects (i.e., are effective).

Most people think herbal medicines are safe to consume in large quantities. I maintain an herb garden and have cured people of flu, body odour, gout, sore throat, dandruff and fungal nail infections using fresh leaves, flowers and roots. Medicinal herbs are effective. Therefore, they are dangerous if misused. An excess of green tea kills beneficial bacteria in the gut and opens the way to an overgrowth of intestinal yeast. This causes flatulence and overall fatigue. Coffee is good for promoting bile flow. People who drink 3 cups of coffee a day are less likely to get gallstones. Too much coffee can bring about high blood pressure.

The motivational strategies in this book all have effects.

Used wisely, they will help your child. Used poorly, they will hurt your child. For example, if you develop an over reliance on physical movement to keep your child on task, you could waste a lot of time and your child might not be able to complete the mastery of the syllabus in time, and thus fail his exams. As another example, if you are unable to calibrate the degree of autonomy that is appropriate for your child when structuring choices, you can actually appear coercive (when you give choices that are too constrained) or your child might choose something you're not ready to accept (when you give choices that are too broadly defined). If you're not careful when setting Impossible Goals (and monitoring their achievement process), you could actually end up with a child who thinks everything is impossible. If you're not careful when sculpting your child's self-concept with positive comments, you could actually end up with a child who won't trust your praises. Both Little Boy and The Daughter have told me before "You're just saying that to make me feel good, Mom. You know it isn't true." I can write about these mistakes because I made many myself, and had many other close calls.

Anything effective (i.e., has effects) is dangerous. It's a

bit like a chemical experiment. If you put too much of a certain chemical, or at the wrong time, the whole thing could explode in your face.

I know for sure that all 11 strategies have effects because all 11 of them have been through 2 layers of validation. The first layer of validation was published psychological research. The 2nd layer of validation was in having used all the strategies myself on my own kids and on other people's kids.

As someone who knows how to conduct psychological research, I am more aware than most that research findings need to be met with some degree of healthy scepticism. What a research paper tells you can be done, may well backfire or have unintended effects when you actually attempt what you learnt in real life. Every piece of research has limitations. I have learnt not to trust research findings blindly. Hence, when I first tried out these strategies, I was careful. In this way, I was able to stop myself or find ways of recovering, whenever something unexpectedly went wrong. I encourage other parents to be careful too. Put every strategy in this book through a common sense screen. Observe carefully for ill effects. Don't overuse any one strategy. Different strategies are appropriate for different situations. It is important to match the right strategy to the situation. Since there are an infinite variety of situations, it is impossible to write them all out in a book like this. Hence, parents must exercise judgment.

Of course, I used these strategies myself and personally experienced their effects. This, in itself, is a limitation as much as it is a strength. It is a strength because the reader knows that these strategies have worked on at least 2 children. It is also a limitation for 2 reasons. Firstly, my children are unique just as all children are unique. Secondly, I am not like any other Mother just like no other Mother is exactly like someone else. The exact family circumstances in which I used these motivation strategies are also different from those that exist in every other family. These are compelling reasons for parents to...

- approach the use of each strategy carefully,
- expect some unpredictability in each strategy's effects,
- be ready to look out for potentially damaging circumstances, and
- be ready to recover situations whenever necessary.

If there is one thing I have learnt, it is that the more I know, the more I realise I don't know. There is still a great deal psychologists need to discover about human motivation. Nonetheless, I do hope that this book will provide parents with a wider range of motivation strategies than they previously knew. There is a lot more one can do to motivate a child apart from bribing, scolding, nagging and punishing. Some of these strategies are vastly more pleasant for both parent and child than bribing, scolding, nagging and punishing. However, do experiment with care, and also do be aware that practice makes perfect.

CONTRADICTORY STRATEGIES

Some readers may have noted that some strategies in this book actually contradict each other. For example, Chapter 1 talks about giving structured choices, but Chapter 11 advises you to use forced goals (i.e., impose a goal). The 2 strategies cannot be used together. This should illustrate clearly that when you have a motivation problem, you should not try and enact every single strategy in this book.

You need to choose the right strategy or the right combination of strategies for the situation. I often run motivation workshops in parent-child pairs. To save time, I accept to train 2 pairs of parent-child at the same time. The 2 parents go away with 2 different sets of strategies because they have different relationships with their children, and their children come with different levels of competence in a given subject. Indeed, the motivation recipe is different depending on whether I am trying to get the children to memorise and recite Chinese, or whether I am trying to get them to do Math worksheets. This is because the nature of the task is different. As you develop skill in these strategies, I hope you will learn to combine them because strategy combination is not inside this book. In the next anecdote, I will describe how 2 sets of parent-child pairs went away from my workshop with 2 very different motivation recipes. The names of the children have been changed.

MIRIAM: A FLAT BATTERY

Miriam attended a Math workshop with her Mom. They had a very strained relationship. Miriam's grades were at borderline pass for all 4 subjects. She was in Primary 5 and her Mother was frantic with worry. The more worried the Mother became, the more controlling she became. She started to pile Miriam with extra drills in every subject, and especially Math. Emotionally, Miriam's

Mother was overwrought. She was anxious, frustrated and angry. The emotional sustenance Miriam's Mother was feeding to her daughter through their EMOTIONAL CONNECTION was highly polluted with negativity.

According to the Mother, Miriam was extremely uncooperative. She would resist all attempts to get her started on any work. She would chase her Mother away from her study desk because she found the large infusions of anxiety so unpleasant. Yet, left alone, Miriam found in herself no motivational energy to stay on task. So, she would get up and walk around, fidget and doodle. Miriam's mother was at her wits' end. The more she worried, the more she nagged. The more she nagged, the more Miriam dragged her feet.

This child's battery was completely flat. She felt like a failure. She wanted to do better but it didn't seem possible because she was bad at every subject. In Math alone, she was poor at simple addition and subtraction.

Miriam's Mother frantically tried to work on every Math skill from complex problem-solving to simple computation at the same time with her child. This overwhelmed both of them – emotional explosions waited to happen at every corner of their days together.

Miriam needed a clear and structured study process which she could independently control (WHOLE TASK – this strategy is one of the strategies not described in this book because there is no space). With a clear process that she could independently manage, she wouldn't feel so controlled by the adults around her, and still be able focus her energies on the step by step behaviours (FOCUS ON PROCESS) that would lead her to success. Miriam's mother did not know how to design study process. She merely nagged Miriam to go and study. This was vague and Miriam, being both weak in the subject and zero on motivational energy was not able to get started, and even if she did start, she couldn't stay on task.

I gave Miriam a very constrained STRUCTURED CHOICE – "Look at this specific Exercise 5.1. Which 2 sums would you like to do?" Next I followed up with a TOO EASY FORCED GOAL because Miriam's battery was flat and needed a highly focused jump-start – "Would you please do 6 sums in this exercise? After every 2 sums, you check the answers okay? If they're wrong, you figure them out and make corrections. When you get both right, come to show me, yes? I will be sitting over there."

Note that both tone and language are warm and soft (EMOTIONAL CONNECTION). I had no prior relationship with the child and so my Emotional Connection with her was small. However, after prolonged exposure to negative energy from Miriam's frustrated Mother, these warm words calmed Miriam and made her feel safe, even though I was actually imposing a TOO EASY FORCED GOAL, without giving her a choice. I didn't allow her to choose which book or which exercise. I imposed Simon Eio's Step-by-Step Math. I only allowed her to choose which 2 sums in the exercise, and I required her to check in with me after every 2 sums (SHORT FEEDBACK LOOP). This short loop gave me the opportunity to use EMOTIONAL CONNECTION with her – infusing her with my joy at her success after every 2 sums. This was meant to top up motivational energy at regular and short intervals. After every 2 sums, I praised her, smiled warmly and patted her shoulder.

Since she had to correct the sums herself, looking at the answers at the back of the book, she was also getting the satisfaction of INFORMATIONAL FEEDBACK with a short FEEDBACK LOOP. The book itself had very clear explanations of the mathematical concepts and it was a book pitched at low levels of difficulty. Miriam was quite capable of learning, doing and correcting 2 sums at a time without help from me.

Frankly, if a parent is good at motivating,

there is no need to learn the syllabus in order to teach. I make sure that Math resources with clear explanations and examples are available. Then I structure a Study Process that the child can use to learn independently. If I took Little Boy's Math exam papers, I would fail. However, I was able to help him score in Math by helping him to interact with good books. Clearly, the approach worked with Miriam too.

Next, the fact that she had to walk to me to show me her work also gave her an opportunity for PHYSICAL MOVEMENT breaking the monotony of the tedious computational practice I had asked of her.

Miriam's Mother never gave choices. She gave orders and her orders were vague. "Go and study." Miriam needed highly constrained STRUCTURED CHOICES embedded within a STUDY PROCESS that her Mother did not know how to design. Miriam's mother learnt to design a simple and clear STUDY PROCESS for Miriam to manage independently. She learnt to use a short FEEDBACK LOOP to give regular top-ups to Miriam's motivational energy. She learnt to give Miriam STRUCTURED CHOICES. Miriam's Mother also needed to repair the EMOTIONAL CONNECTION with her daughter so that she could feed her daughter positive emotions throughout their hours of working together. After observing me during the workshop, and receiving specific feedback about her tone, her words, her body language and her gestures, Miriam's Mother made some progress in altering her own responses to her child. Their work together became more pleasant, and Miriam was more willing to do Math practices thereafter. I tend to believe that when a child is not motivated, it is not the child's fault. It is the parent's.

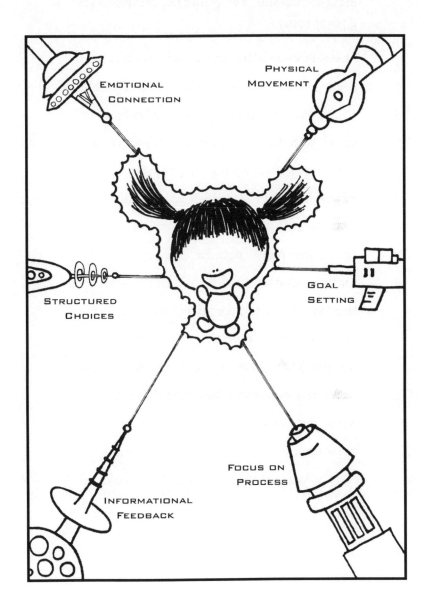

HELEN: ONE WHO WON'T ACCEPT CHALLENGE

Helen attended the same Math workshop as Miriam. Helen was a very bright child with a strong Math foundation. Her grades hovered in the high 80s and low 90s. Her relationship with her Mother was warm and close. However, Helen's mother complained that Helen would always choose easy Math over challenging Math. Since Helen was bright, her Mother was keen to stretch her child enough to give her a shot at the perfect score of 100%, in Math. Naturally, Helen's Mother assigned her daughter a fair amount of challenging problem sums, which her daughter hated to do.

I asked Helen's Mother to procure an easy Step-by-Step Math practice book by Simon Eio, and Visible Thinking by Ammiel Wan. Then I provided to Helen a STRUCTURED CHOICE that was much broader than what I had given Miriam.

Me: What do you think of these 2 books?

Little Helen: Ammiel Wan's book is more difficult because it is a lot like IQ Math. Simon Eio's book is like normal Math, so it is quite easy.

Me: Which would you like to do?

Little Helen: The easy one.

Me: That's fine but here is a bit of wisdom I will share with you. If you still want to do the easy book, that's fine. It's really up to you. If you do the easy book, you'll have to do the difficult book later. But if you think you can do the difficult book and show me you can, then there is no sense to go back to do the easy book. It's just like asking you to do kindergarten handwriting practice when I already know you can write. I'll get Mommy to throw away the easy book.

Helen: I still want the easy book... errrrr... hmmmm... no... I want the difficult book.

Me: Ok. You're a clever girl. This way, you will do less work. But you do know that if you can't handle the difficult book, you will have to complete both books. You can only skip one book if you show me that you can manage the difficult one.

Helen: I can try to handle the difficult one.

In the above conversation, I had applied another strategy not described in this book – REGULAR REINFORCEMENT. I build this strategy into every work schedule. Play is rewarding to the child. If Helen knew that doing difficult work always exempted her from doing a large volume of easy work, she would be motivated to choose the challenging tasks.

Next, I set up a FEEDBACK LOOP that was slightly longer than what I had set up for Miriam, and a somewhat more complex STUDY PROCESS. I asked Helen to (1) read the explanation in Ammiel Wan's book, (2) choose the most difficult sum (STRUCTURED CHOICE) from each of the 3 sub-units of a chapter, do them, (3) mark them (INFORMATIONAL FEEDBACK) and ensure they were correct, before coming to show me (WHOLE TASK). I also asked Helen to choose (STRUCTURED CHOICE) the chapter she wanted to do whilst laying down the boundary condition that it had to be a topic that her school had never taught. Then I left her alone to work. Like with Miriam, I required that she walk to me to show me her work (PHYSICAL MOVEMENT).

Every time she showed me her work, I provided positive comments (SPECIFY-AND-MAGNIFY): (1) You are so clever. Teacher has not taught this and you can do this very difficult sum. (2) It must have felt good to get this difficult sum right without being taught. (3) You are much better at Math than I thought you were. (4) You have some talent in Math (DESIGN THE SELF-CONCEPT™). By the end of the chapter, Helen was on a motivational energy high. She had just achieved a series of challenging goals (that weren't too easy and weren't too hard). She had had the satisfaction of making nice ticks next to her answers (INFORMATIONAL FEEDBACK). She felt trusted and in control (WHOLE TASK) because she was allowed to pick the most difficult sum in each sub-unit (STRUCTURED CHOICES). The degree of challenge, whilst high, was well calibrated to her intellectual ability (CHALLENGE STRESS – also not covered in this book). I had specifically commented on aspects of her performance and personality (SPECIFY-AND-MAGNIFY).

It was time to hit her with an IMPOSSIBLE GOAL.

I produced a Primary 5 book and said "Helen, you're in Primary 4 right? This is a Primary 5 book. If you can't handle this, it's ok. If you can, it's a bonus. If you try and you fail, you will learn something (LEARNING GOAL ORIENTATION). If you try and you succeed, it will be a bonus. Do you want to try (STRUCTURED CHOICE)?"

Helen nodded her head. Halfway through, she ran into problems. She was stuck. I told her that she could stop anytime she wanted and go back to Primary 4 work (STRUCTURED CHOICE). She refused. It was at this point that Helen's Mother's eyeballs fell out. She had never seen her daughter take on a challenge like this before, and actually choose not to give up.

I waited patiently for Helen whilst she figured her way through the sub-unit by re-reading and by thinking hard. I sat next to her and allowed my calm patience to encourage her through the very small EMOTIONAL CONNECTION we shared. When she finally succeeded, she was overjoyed because she had just done some Primary 5 work all by herself.

One week later, Helen's mother wrote me a note saying that Helen discovered that day how enjoyable conquering challenges can be. Of course, whatever little attitudinal change I was able to effectuate in Helen would disappear if Helen's Mother did not know the strategies for maintaining the new attitude in her child. Helen's Mother was a quick study

herself. Once she grasped the strategies and observed how I behaved when implementing the strategies, she was able to go home and work with her child. The biggest mistakes Helen's Mother made were (1) exposing her child to highly challenging work without giving the child a choice, (2) exposing her child to too many failure experiences with challenging problems without priming for LEARNING GOAL ORIENTATION, (3) failing to top up motivational energy with encouragement through the EMOTIONAL CONNECTION.

The above 2 anecdotes are meant to illustrate how the individual strategies need to be chosen specially for the situation. They also need to be specifically combined for specific situations. Someone like me, with a deep knowledge of Human Motivation (my PhD alone was 7 long years of reading, research and practice) can read situations and develop motivation recipes flexibly and fast. If you don't know how to do that, it's fine. Most parents have 1 or 2 children only. You just need to figure out over time and with some experimentation, the motivation recipe that will work with your child. However, as you experiment, be mindful that there are dangers.

I do have to apologise that I have not put down every strategy I know in this book. Firstly, reviewers accused me already of writing too long a book. Secondly, I cannot put down more than 2 decades of experience into a book like this. Thirdly, I only realised that strategies were missing when I wrote the anecdotes on Miriam and Helen. In the workshops, I naturally enact the necessary strategies. I do this almost unconsciously because my familiarity with Human Motivation reaches beyond theory and research. It has become an integral part of who I am. However, I do hope that what is in here is already useful enough.

MASTER YOURSELF COMPLETELY

As you can see from the anecdotes, many of the above strategies require parents to behave very differently than what they have been used to doing. Some of our gestures and words when we interact with our children escape conscious control. To be able to use these strategies properly, parents must master not only what they are conscious of, but also what they unconsciously say and do.

Children are extraordinarily sensitive to what is unsaid – a tightness in the tone, an absent-minded frown are sometimes enough to contaminate an interaction enough to render a strategy ineffective.

THINK ABOUT ETHICS

These strategies are not limited in their use on children. Indeed, I have adapted all of them from research in work motivation – i.e., the initial targets of research were often adults. For example, Designing the Self-Concept was adapted from a similar strategy often used by charismatic organisational leaders, who link a proposed course of action to the self-concepts of their followers. For example, Captain Barbossa in Pirates of the Caribbean 3 motivated his sailors to brave death at Whitecap Bay by saying "Are ye King's men?!" In so doing, Captain Barbossa was telling his men "If you see yourself as a King's soldier (i.e., if that is your self-concept), then braving death is what King's soldiers do." Even a layman can feel the motivation of the moment when watching the movie. No wonder, because in the absence of everything else that motivates, people will behave in ways consistent with their self-concepts. If I am a King's soldier then I will die for my king for no other reason than that it is what I think I was born to do.

Was it right for Captain Barbossa to appeal to men's self-concepts so successfully, and to later abandon them to their deaths at the hands of the mermaids in White Cap Bay? There are ethical considerations therefore, in the use of all the motivation strategies in this book.

Did I do the right thing in using Specify-and-Magnify to motivate my undergraduate students so thoroughly that one student spent his parent's hard earned money to rent a business suit just to make his project presentation? See this anecdote in Chapter 12 on Specify-and-Magnify. Did I do the right thing in motivating Little Boy to study so hard that he would willingly choose to study on Sundays too? Would I be doing the right thing if I used all the tricks in my book to motivate The Daughter to stay in Singapore for her university studies? Am I doing the right thing when I consciously say and do things that will motivate The Husband to buy me a diamond bracelet for our 20th wedding anniversary?

I don't suppose there are easy answers to such questions. It is one thing if you succeed at doing all the above without really knowing how. It is quite another when you consciously set out to do all the above using logical thinking and precision planning processes that most people associate with planning a war. People who learn to use these strategies gain power over others. With this power, comes responsibility. How far can one go before motivation becomes manipulation?

Little Boy is forbidden from doing any work on Sundays because I consider that every child has an unalienable right to play. I don't care that he wants to work on Sundays. The reason he wants to work on Sundays, is because I knew how to make him want it. Hence, I am responsible, and I have to prevent him from hurting himself with too much studying. For ethical considerations too, I wouldn't allow The Husband to buy me a diamond bracelet for our 20th wedding anniversary in order to protect his wallet.

I do the above to stay within the boundaries of what I think is an ethical framework. I also do the above because I know that trust lies at the foundation of each strategy's effectiveness. Unless the individual trusts you, none of the strategies will work. Hence, I go to great lengths to ensure that the well-being of my children come before my own self-pride in their achievements. If I think that going for gold will damage their health or their character development, I will forego the gold. If the price of a top score is to be paid with sweatshop hours, then I will forego that top score. I am but a steward of my children's lives. Their lives are not mine to use for my own pleasures. This must be clear to all parents who learn to use these strategies. Use them well and use them to ensure your child's well-being, not your own pleasure. If you don't use these strategies ethically, your children will learn to distrust you and when you are old and grey, it is you who will lose out.

These strategies were written for parents but anyone who has care of children can use them too. Teachers will find these strategies useful. I know I use them all the time with the people I teach, and I have taught people of all ages from 1 year old to 75 years old. Age doesn't matter. What matters is knowing when and how to use these strategies. What matters is also knowing when to pack away these strategies and not use them at all, because using them constitutes unethical behaviour.

These strategies are tools. They are no different from a hammer. You can use a hammer to break a window to steal things, or you can use a hammer to build a house. Hopefully, the reader will only use the hammer to build a

house, and refuse to use it when it comes to having to break a window to steal things.

WHAT ABOUT WORKING MOTHERS / FATHERS?

When I wrote this book, I organised the strategies by research streams. This means that each strategy chapter drew inspiration from a single stream of motivation research. In this way, I made sure that I covered the few major streams of motivation research that I had found most useful for my children. I did not write this book for any one type of parent: working or non-working. As such, all the strategies are jumbled up and not presented in a way that is friendly to working mothers/fathers.

The most common question from those who come for One-to-Pair Motivation Therapy™ and who work full-time, is the time investment these strategies require. I would be lying if I wrote that igniting your child's internal drive requires no face time at all. You do need to have daily face time with your child in order to effectuate these strategies.

Some strategies require your physical presence right through the task. **IMPOSSIBLE GOALS** is one such strategy. You can't leave the child to attempt the impossible on his own. On the other hand, **DESIGN THE SELF-CONCEPT**™ can be done on the phone and over dinner. **TOO EASY GOALS** can be a way of getting work done in the parent's absence. **STRUCTURED CHOICES** can be done on Sunday afternoons when you sit down with the child to work out the tasks for the whole week. Little Boy and I work out tasks for a month and a half at a time.

These strategies both take up time in the short-term, and save you time and effort in the long-term.

References

1. Festinger, L. and J.M. Carlsmith, *Cognitive consequences of forced compliance.* Journal of Abnormal and Social Psychology, 1959. **58**: p. 203-210.

2. Hobfoll, S.E., *The influence of culture, community, and the nested-self in the stress process: Advancing conservation of resources theory.* Applied Psychology: An International Review, 2001. **50**: p. 337-421.

3. Williams, G.C., et al., *Motivational predictors of weight loss and weight loss maintenance.* Journal of Personality and Social Psychology, 1996. **70**: p. 115-126.

4. Grolnick, W.S. and R.M. Ryan, *Parent styles associated with associated with children's self-regulation and competence in school.* Journal of Educational Psychology, 1989. **81**: p. 143-154.

5. Sheldon, K.M. and A.J. Elliot, *Goal striving, need satisfaction, and longitudinal well-being: The self-concordance model.* Journal of Personality and Social Psychology, 1999. **76**: p. 482-497.

6. Hollenbeck, J.R., C.R. Williams, and H.J. Klein, *An empirical examination of the antecedents of commitment to difficult goals.* Journal of Applied Psychology, 1989. **74**: p. 18-23.

7. Locke, E.A., *The motivation to work: What we know,* in

Advances in motivation and achievement, M. Maehr and P.R. Pintrich, Editors. 1997, JAI Press: Greenwich, CT. p. 375-412.

8. Luthans, F. and R. Kreitner, *The Role of Punishment in Organizational Behavior Modification.* Public Personnel Management, 1973. **2**: p. 156-161.

9. Latham, G.P., *Work motivation: History, theory, research and practice.* 2007, Thousand Oaks, CA: Sage Publications, Inc.

10. Wood, R.E. and A. Bandura, *Social cognitive theory of organizational management.* Academy of Management Review, 1989. **14**: p. 361-384.

11. Bannister, R., *The four-minute mile.* 1955, New York: Lyons Press.

12. Piper, W., *The little engine that could.* 1930, New York: Platt & Munk.

13. Vandewalle, D., W.L. Cron, and J.W. Slocum Jr., *The role of goal orientation following performance feedback.* Journal of Applied Psychology, 2001. **86**: p. 629-640.

14. Weatherford, J., *The Secret History of the Mongol Queens.* Vol. New York. 2010: Crown Publishers.

15. Steele, C.M., *The psychology of self-affirmation: Sustaining the integrity of the self,* in *Advances in experimental social psychology,* L. Berkowitz, Editor. 1988, Academic Press: New York. p. 261-302.

16. Myers, D.G., *Social Psychology*. 2008, New York: McGraw-Hill.

17. Baumeister, R.F., *Self-regulation and ego threat: Motivated cognition, self-deception, and destructive goal-setting*, in *The Psychology of action*, P. Gollwitzer and J. Bargh, Editors. 1996, Guilford Press: New York. p. 27-47.

18. Locke, E.A. and G.P. Latham, *Building a practically useful theory of goal setting and task motivation: A 35 year odyssey*. American Psychologist, 2002. **57**: p. 705-717.

19. Watkins, J.M. and B.J. Mohr, *Appreciative inquiry: Change at the speed of imagination*. 2001, San Francisco: Jossey-Bass.

20. Ryan, R.M. and C.M. Frederick, *On energy, personality, and health: Subjective vitality as a dynamic reflection of well-being*. Journal of Personality, 1997. **65**: p. 529-565.

21. Dutton, D. and A.P. Aron, *Some evidence for heightened sexual attraction under conditions of high anxiety*. Journal of Personality and Social psychology, 1974. **28**: p. 94-100.

Acknowledgements

I want to thank my reviewers – Ren Yuh, Li Lin, Seth, Shi Cheng, Ai Lanne, Leah, Ting Ting, Wen Shan and Stephanie. Each of them was able to gently articulate what they did not like about the initial drafts of the book, whilst demonstrating enthousiasm about the book topic and the small insights it had provided them. In this way, I was both helped to improve and encouraged to continue and see my book project through to its end.

I owe a special thanks to Clara Li who was indefatigable in her pursuit of excellence when making illustrations for the book, and designing the overall look and feel of it. She saw blemishes where I saw none and she spent hours fixing the blemishes. I am so honoured to have her drawings in my book.

I would like to give special thanks also to Jackie of KHL Printing Co Pte Ltd for his patience and brilliant customer service.

14682631R00190

Printed in Great Britain
by Amazon.co.uk, Ltd.,
Marston Gate.